Reconciliation

A Journey

Michael Gordon is the national editor of the *Age* newspaper in Melbourne. A former political editor of *The Australian* and New York correspondent for the Melbourne *Herald*, he has also worked as sports editor and chief of staff at the *Age* and as deputy editor of the *Sunday Age*. He is a graduate in commerce at Melbourne University. His biography of Paul Keating, *A Question of Leadership*, was published in 1993 and updated in 1996 as *A True Believer*.

Books published in the ⓇEPORTAGE series

REPORTAGE

MICHAEL GORDON

RECONCILIATION
A Journey

UNSW
PRESS

A UNSW Press book

Published by
University of New South Wales Press Ltd
University of New South Wales
UNSW Sydney NSW 2052
AUSTRALIA
www.unswpress.com.au

National Library of Australia
Cataloguing-in-Publication entry:

Gordon, Michael, 1955– .
Reconciliation: a journey.
Includes index.
ISBN 0 86840 596 5.

1. Aborigines, Australian — Australia, Northern —
Social conditions. 2. Aborigines, Australian — Australia,
Northern — Social life and customs. 3. Australia,
Northern — Description and travel. I. Title. (Series: Reportage
(Sydney, N.S.W.)).

306.0899915

Cover photograph Lucinda James by Michael Gordon
Printer BPA

Contents

To Harry, mate and mentor

Preface

John Howard was an unlikely catalyst for the journey that resulted in this book. Back in December 1996, I was among the journalists at the prime minister's end-of-year press conference. In the course of discussing the issue of reconciliation, someone asked if he was intending to visit Aboriginal communities. Mr Howard said yes, he did intend to visit them, but not in any tokenistic sense. He then made a remark that struck a chord with me and, I suspect, several others in the room: 'Like all Australians who in their upbringing have not had much contact with Aboriginal people, and I guess like many others I didn't, I have a lot to learn and understand about their culture'.

It was a simple and honest statement. It made me reflect on my own life experience and my lack of contact with Aboriginal Australia. At school in the leafy Melbourne suburb of Kew, I had walked to raise money for Abschol, a scholarship scheme for Aborigines. But I was not taught the place of the first Australians in the story of our nation's history, or anything of their culture. As a political journalist, there were many opportunities to meet Aboriginal leaders in the course of covering a variety of issues. I had come to know and respect a number of them and I would later travel with Gatjil Djerrkura in rural New South Wales in 1999. But even then my experience remained narrow and selective.

The opportunity to change this came in 2000, the last year of Australia's first formal process of reconciliation. I proposed to my editor at *The Age*, Michael Gawenda, that I travel extensively in black Australia and prepare a series of articles ahead of the 'Corroboree 2000' event in Sydney in May, an event that was intended to be the climax of ten years of work by the Council for Aboriginal Reconciliation. The aim was to address many of the issues that would be tackled in the council's final documents and recommendations. Michael agreed and I set off in March.

The series was published in the week leading up to Corroboree 2000, but my journey was not over. It continued at Corroboree 2000, when an estimated 250 000 people walked for reconciliation across the Sydney Harbour Bridge, at the Olympic Games, at the Melbourne walk in December, and at the handover of the council's final report four days later. This book is a personal account of what became a watershed year in the country's journey of reconciliation.

Acknowledgments

This book was made possible by Michael Gawenda's leadership, and the assistance of a great many people, particularly Brian Johnstone, who helped in planning the trip and suggesting contacts along the way.

I would also like to thank Smiley Johnson, Alastair Harris, Andrea Collins, Chips Mackinolty, Kathy Rioli and Paul Lane. The names of others deserving thanks will be clear to readers. There were many others who provided insights before I left and in the preparation of this book, including Noel Pearson, Evelyn Scott, Sir Gustav Nossal, Olga Havnen, Ian Spicer, Linda Burney, Bob Collins, Brian Aarons and politicians on both sides of federal politics. Special thanks to Leigh Henningham at *The Age*, and the staffs of the libraries at *The Age* and Parliament House.

Thanks also to Peter Browne from UNSW Press for approaching me with the idea of developing my work into a book, James Drown for editing the manuscript, and my family for being part of this journey.

Introduction

Our nation must have the courage to own the truth, to heal the wounds of the past so that we can move on together at peace with ourselves. From the *Declaration Towards Reconciliation*, May 2000

'Are you going to tell the truth?'

It sounded more like a challenge than a question. It came from an Aboriginal woman on Mornington Island, a community mourning the loss of four young men who had taken their own lives in as many months.

Are you going to tell the truth? I struggled with that question in the following weeks, usually during bouts of sleeplessness in places I had never been and probably would never see again. I came to realise that there were four layers of truth about the state of Australia's first people. To stop at the first layer is as dangerous and deceptive as to tell a lie.

The first layer is what I saw with the naked eye, especially in remote Australia: indigenous Australians living in Third World conditions, where decades of passive welfare and substance abuse have so numbed their spirits that there is now a lost generation to follow those who were stolen. This is a generation so dysfunctional and lacking in spark that some well-meaning people, black and white, consider that the most prudent course is to focus on the children, the next generation.

In Darwin early in the year 2000, a 20-year-old from the Tiwi Islands could not be questioned after being arrested because he could not speak English. The policeman did the right thing. He called in an interpreter who discovered the man's Tiwi was worse than his English. What future does he have?

The first layer of truth is everywhere. I have visited places where domestic violence is endemic, where life expectancy for men is in the

1

low 40s, where sexual health is several times worse than in mainstream Australia, where almost half the adult population suffers from diabetes and the vast majority have skin infections, where 40 per cent of newborn babies are under-nourished, where 16- and 17-year-olds leave the school system with the literacy skills of an average white five-year-old, where squalid, hopelessly overcrowded living conditions are benignly accepted and where, most ominously of all, suicide comes in dark waves that are increasing in size and frequency.

Why the suicides? Kerry Arabena, then the director of the Apunipima Cape York Health Council, offered a simple explanation. She said most of the Aboriginal men who kill themselves do so out of desperation. And the young? 'It's their inability to hate', she said. 'They love so much, they'd prefer to lose their lives than to continue without it.'

Love? Love is such a debased commodity in some of these places that it is measured by a readiness to part with cash so that a husband or wife or child can buy alcohol or drugs or gamble. The result is an epidemic in a form of extortion: 'Give me the money or I'll kill myself'.

In one Tiwi Island community, suicide attempts are so common that barbed-wire 'crowns of thorns' have been attached to all power poles to prevent teenage boys and young men climbing them and threatening to throw themselves on the live power lines. Police were called out to 50 suicide attempts in 12 months and the local power supply was shut down more than 40 times in 1999 after young men and boys had climbed the poles.

All too often it is the more gifted and successful who succeed in taking their lives. Titjikala is a small community 120 kilometres from Alice Springs where two of the most promising young people committed suicide in 1999. Why? Because they couldn't cope with the pressures and the barriers placed in their way. 'Young suicides aren't coming from the no-hopers', says Harry Scott, Titjikala's white community adviser. 'It's from those who feel and think.'

Alcohol abuse, long considered to be a symptom of the problems afflicting so many communities, is now a major cause of them. It has been for some time. I have been to many places where VB (known as 'Violent Bitter') rules, where the most important decision couples make each week is how to divide their welfare or work-for-the-dole cheque between the three Gs: grog, ganga and gambling. Respect, responsibility and discipline — the foundations of traditional indigenous culture — are now alien concepts.

A coronial inquiry in the Northern Territory late in 1999 was told that 98 per cent of police work on the Tiwi Islands was alcohol-related, and that if the licensed outlets were removed there would be little justification for much of the police presence on the islands. After limits were placed on the sale of full-strength beer on days when welfare cheques arrive in Wilcannia, in western New South Wales, early in 2000, the hospital reported a 60 per cent drop in serious assaults.

Then there is the case of Mornington Island, where the licensed canteen was closed for 11 days late in 1999 after five islanders, including some of the community's most respected leaders, were killed in a plane crash. According to the local police sergeant, John Herbert, not a single offence was committed while the pub was closed. Ironically, the only disturbance was when a group of women protested against an early re-opening of the canteen.

A banned substance in Aboriginal communities for most of this century, alcohol has so corrupted the culture of sharing that individuals are now expected to share grog and share the money needed to buy it. The right to drink that came with the passage of the 1967 referendum has, in many communities, led to the denial of the rights of women and children.

Initially, it was only men who drank. Now, the expansion to women of what prominent Aboriginal lawyer Noel Pearson has called the 'drinking circle' is largely to blame for a collapse in parental values and responsibility. As Pearson put it: 'It's no wonder kids petrol sniff if both their parents are drunk'.

No-one, of course, forced Aborigines to drink when the prohibition was lifted. But a study undertaken for Cape York Health Council early in 2000 details the level of pressure the Queensland Government placed on communities to open beer canteens in the 1960s, 1970s and 1980s, often against their wishes. And the most likely motive? The report's author, Geoff Genever, concluded: 'I believe that beer canteens were seen as a source of income that would pay for infrastructure and development, thereby relieving the burden on the state purse'.

The trouble with the first layer of truth is that it invites the stereotype that is grossly unfair to the many who refuse to conform to it. Everywhere I have been, from Wilcannia to Palm Island, from Doomadgee to Broome, I have met people, young and old, who were determined to make things better, who shone like beacons and pursued a simple Australian dream: that Aborigines and Torres Strait

Islanders should be able to have their culture and succeed in mainstream society. People such as Grayson Williams, a member of the Woomera dance group, who devotes his energy to promoting culture in a community where traditional song and dance was prohibited by order of the missionaries in the 1940s. Or Auntie Hilyer Jonny, who, without any assistance, started a shelter for abused women and children in her own home at Doomadgee, regularly placing herself between those she was protecting and their drunk and violent partners.

In many places, these people are assisted by non-indigenous Australians, including those of the police who are breaking down barriers and reducing crime in places like Bourke, Brewarrina and Moree in western New South Wales, where the gungis (police) now play the murris (Aborigines) in an annual touch football match.

But all too often those who want to make a difference are swimming against the tide, hamstrung by the second layer of truth. This second layer is a conspiracy of abdication, mostly unwitting but sometimes deliberate, by governments big and small, by bureaucracies, by administrators and by leaders, white and black. It shows itself in state-of-the-art hospitals built but inadequately staffed; in old-age facilities situated in the wrong places, with more beds than are required; in sporting organisations that find reasons to exclude indigenous community teams from their competitions and so compound their lack of motivation; in good programs not followed through because of overlapping jurisdictions and high turnover of staff; in bad programs imposed without consultation or the slightest sensitivity to indigenous protocols and culture; and in those local leaders, black and white, who refuse to surrender power or exercise it for the greater good. Noel Pearson put it more eloquently, saying 'Aboriginal affairs is littered with scenes of horses without saddles, of cows with bridles'.

Black politics, especially at the local level, can be practised with a raw intensity. Allegations of nepotism and cronyism are common. There are also leaders who tolerate the 'sly groggers' — those who sell alcohol for massive profits and soak up the welfare cheques of the drinkers. Then there are those who simply do not see the urgency to change, or who are so inured to the problems that they regard them as normal.

The third layer of truth is the history of the treatment of Aboriginal Australians. Two centuries of this history have largely eluded 'mainstream' Australia. This has left us with the twin legacies of inter-generational trauma and indigenous loss of memory. The mistake many make is to assume the traumas ended when the massacres stopped, or when the last children were forcibly removed from their parents.

Barbara Flick, who was working to lift health standards in western New South Wales, borrowed a metaphor from her father to describe the impact of history on the songs, languages and corroborees of some communities. He saw Australia as a jigsaw, blown apart by the wind of white invasion. 'For 200 years we've being trying to put the puzzle back together', she said. The task of reconciliation is all the harder because too many pieces have been irretrievably lost.

Kathy Rioli, sister of Essendon footballer Michael Long, talked of feeling too shamed to dance in an Aboriginal ceremony because both her parents were stolen from their country and culture. She grew up in a kind of halfway house between indigenous culture and white society. Francene George, of Yirrkala, spoke of being too embarrassed as a young woman to reveal she grew up on Palm Island, the community founded as a penal colony for 'troublesome Aborigines'.

The final layer of truth is prejudice. It continues to assert itself in many forms, from mandatory sentencing laws that mean Aborigines are jailed in disproportionate numbers for trivial offences; to the shopkeepers who serve black people last; to the taxi drivers who charge them exorbitant fares, especially for 'grog runs'; to the more insidious and institutional discrimination that sees young and willing workers overlooked by employers too influenced by the stereotype of indolence and alcohol abuse.

Even in Moree, a once-divided city now leading the way on reconciliation — where progress is reflected in the black faces serving at Woolworths, the declining crime rate and the increase in 'real jobs' in cotton and other industries — some old attitudes die hard. There is the woman who insists it is not racist to despise the juveniles who are the main cause of crime. Why? 'Because they are not a race. They are a breed, like fleas and ticks', she told me. Hers is the extreme voice of a small minority, but it represents a constituency capable of wielding influence at the ballot box. Pauline Hanson's One Nation proved that.

This also helps explain Irving Saulwick's summary of a focus-group discussion with Aborigines in Moree for the Council for Aboriginal Reconciliation: 'The anger among this group was palpable. It arose from a feeling not only of dispossession but of continuing comprehensive discrimination which touched virtually every aspect of their lives and reached back down the generations as far as anyone could remember. It was so deep-seated that every action by non-Aboriginal people or institutions, however benign that action might have appeared, was viewed through a prism of anger, and interpreted in the most cynical way.'

Then there is the other side of racism. At the Granites Gold Mine in the Western Desert region of central Australia, I met an Aboriginal man who had moved out of his community in Alice Springs because he could not abide the racism of a couple of individuals who lived there.

These layers of truth are central to the issue of reconciliation.

The only sentence that survived verbatim from the original draft declaration for reconciliation to the final version launched at Corroboree 2000 in Sydney in May 2000 says this: 'Our nation must have the courage to own the truth, to heal the wounds of the past so that we can move on together at peace with ourselves'. It is also there in the draft that John Howard wanted the Council for Reconciliation to embrace. But before we can own the truth, we need to seek it out, all four layers of it, and accept it.

It won't be easy. The prime minister complained early in 2000 that Australians never heard the good news stories about indigenous people or the progress being made to address profound disadvantage. Up to a point, he was right. He was able to itemise several areas, particularly in employment and training, where progress has been made. Perhaps the clearest example was a three-fold increase in the number of indigenous students involved in vocational education and training in the ten years to 1998.

But it is also the case that stories of increasing disadvantage often fail to penetrate, at least partly because many remote communities are simply out of sight and out of mind. Recent reports detailing a crisis in indigenous education in the Northern Territory, revealing the extent of petrol sniffing in remote communities, and escalating domestic violence in Queensland communities are just three examples. The Women's Task Force Report on Violence in Queensland reported an increase in the number of violent and sexual offences and breaches of domestic orders from 664 in 1994 to 1075 in 1998. 'The harsh reality is that many families are now trapped in environments where deviance and atrocities have become accepted as normal behaviour', the report found.

Despite a 51 per cent increase in health spending by the Howard Government since 1996, coupled with a willingness to back indigenous health services, blindness still occurs up to ten times more frequently in indigenous people than in other Australians; they have four times the incidence of coronary heart disease; and in the 20 to 50 age group, more than ten times the prevalence of diabetes. In education, although Howard pointed to a four-fold increase in Year Twelve retention rates from 8.6 per cent in the mid-1970s to 33 per cent, this was really no more than an informed punt. National figures have only been available since 1994, when the national retention rate was 32.5 per cent.

Even where the Federal Government has initiated action, such as the case of indigenous eye health, progress has been frustratingly slow. The Health Minister, Dr Michael Wooldridge, commissioned a study in 1997 by the head of Melbourne University's department of ophthalmology, Professor Hugh Taylor. Taylor found that, in some places the prevalence and intensity of trachoma — the slowly blinding eye infection — remained as severe as when he had toured the same areas working with the late Professor Fred Hollows 20 years previously. He also examined the serious and growing problem of diabetes.

Although Wooldridge accepted Taylor's 17 recommendations, and Howard announced funding to implement one of them during his only visit to an Aboriginal community in 1998, Taylor says little has really changed. 'Basically these recommendations have at best been incompletely implemented, and at worst not', he said in March 2000, describing the experience as a salutary lesson on the extent of inertia within bureaucracies, federal and state.

'I live in a house that's got hot and cold running water and electricity and a garbage collection', Taylor said, 'and you can only imagine what it's like for the Aboriginal people and Torres Strait Islanders in these remote communities. They hear all these good words and see all these do-gooding whites coming through, and not a damn thing changes. That's just got to be devastating, day after day, year after year. No wonder people get angry.'

Michael Gordon

Once a week the children of St Therese's Community School, Wilcannia, are treated to Weet-bix for breakfast.

1 '60 Minutes' in Wilcannia

A community like Wilcannia is grieving so bad. Nobody knows it but people like us, who have been there and seen it. There's a death there every two or three weeks. I mean, these people are bleeding inside. Smiley Johnson, Broken Hill

Unless the white man turns around, acknowledges his mistakes, comes clean, and then sets about genuinely and sincerely rectifying the problems, we're just going to stay as is. It's always going to be an itch that you can't scratch, a thorn in your side. Jack Scott, Bourke

You make advances, then you take steps back and then you go through deep valleys. If I was just here to see results, I don't think I'd be here. Sister Margaret McGrath, Wilcannia

The reality is that things are happening and somebody's got to speak up. Alison Johnson, Griffith

The other thing about the truth is who tells it, how they tell it and, most importantly, whether they embellish it to make their point. If a family, or a community, has a deep, dark secret that needs to be brought out into the open, there is more chance of a positive reception if it is a member of that family or someone who has the family's trust who tells the truth. My experience in Wilcannia, a depressed Aboriginal community in far-western New South Wales, became a case study in what can happen when the truth is overstated by an outsider, even one with noble intentions, and televised to a national audience.

I began my journey in Wilcannia partly because Linda Burney, the chairperson of the New South Wales Council for Reconciliation, told me of Heidi Bugmy, an Aboriginal girl who in 1999 became the first student, black or white, in Wilcannia Central's 105-year history to complete Year Twelve. In February, I spoke to the school's headmaster, Canadian-born James Hackett, and he seemed receptive to the idea of a visit. We talked for a long time over the phone and it was impossible not to be struck by his commitment, and impressed by the school's progress, which was reflected in improved results and attendance, and a greater level of parental involvement, admittedly from a very low base.

But there was one potential problem. Hackett explained that any approval for a visit would have to come from the Education Department's PR man, Grant Hatch, who in turn told me that '60 Minutes' was already planning a story on Heidi and the school. There were other schools with good stories to tell, he said. 'Why not pick one of them?'

I tried to reach an accommodation with '60 Minutes' producer, Alex Hodgkinson, but failed. When she finally returned my calls, her message was blunt: the town (or the story) wasn't big enough for the both of us, even though it eventually became clear we would be there in different weeks, I would be alone and my series of articles would probably appear after the '60 Minutes' story.

It made no difference that Ray Martin, a member of the Council for Aboriginal Reconciliation who was returning to his former life as '60 Minutes' reporter, had already told Australia of Heidi's achievement in a column in the *Sydney Morning Herald*. Martin's column appeared opposite the editorial page and prompted a Sydney Sunday paper to visit Wilcannia the following weekend to report on Heidi's achievement. But it was also a pointer to the problems that would follow several months later. Martin's article began:

A remarkable thing happened in Wilcannia last year. An Aboriginal girl passed the Higher School Certificate. In that troubled, wild west town she's the first to do it. Boy or girl. She's become a fantastic role model. One understandably proud teacher told me: 'If a girl reaches 18 around here without getting her front teeth knocked out or falling pregnant, or both, it's a minor miracle'. They have to deal in miracles out Wilcannia way.

After several more phone calls to '60 Minutes' producer and no progress, I agreed to bypass the school, deciding instead to divide my first week between a number of towns in western New South Wales. I had no choice.

I arrived at Broken Hill on a Monday night, having flown in from Melbourne, via Adelaide. I had arranged to call William 'Smiley' Johnson when I landed. He suggested we meet at one of the town's Italian restaurants. Johnson was then the regional director of

the Maari Ma Health Aboriginal Corporation and had been suggested as one with an insight into the problems facing communities like
Wilcannia. His friend, Michael Stewart, a former head of the New
South Wales Department of Aboriginal Affairs, came with him.
Johnson is a big, unpretentious man, who seemed as open as a book.
Soon he was outlining his vision for tackling disadvantage by
empowering regional bodies to find their own solutions, rather than
have them imposed by government and layers of bureaucracy. 'One
of the biggest cures for Aboriginal ill-health is employment', he said.
'If we can give our people some real jobs, if they're in work, then
they're not at the pub abusing their bodies, are they?'

But he also underscored the complexity of the problem, and told
me matter-of-factly, 'Most policies on Aboriginal health are all about
the physical stuff — housing, water, sewerage. There's nothing much
about your emotional well-being, what's between your eyes. A community like Wilcannia is grieving so bad. Nobody knows it but people like us, who have been there and seen it. There's a death there
every two or three weeks. I mean, these people are bleeding inside.'

He explained how working parties had been set up in several
communities, including Wilcannia, with the aim of making the
agencies more responsive to real needs. 'The idea is that we don't
have to take any more what the government wants to give us. If we
don't like it, tell them to come back with something you really want,
not have something imposed on you.' The Wilcannia working group
would be meeting later that week and he invited me to attend.

I mentioned my problem with '60 Minutes'. Smiley just smiled,
saying his sister Alison worked at the school as the only black teacher.
He was sure she'd be happy to have a talk. After all, he said, they
couldn't tell her what to do in her own time. He was wrong.

We chatted for more than an hour, the conversation turning finally to the prospects for reconciliation. Smiley's assessment was not
optimistic. 'I think it's a long way off', he said. He would like non-
Aboriginal people to put themselves in the Aboriginal position, 'to be
a blackfella for a day, and to feel the hurt and the emotion and the
stuff we know goes on. We don't want them to love us or whatever,
just to understand what it's like. If they were in Aboriginal shoes, they
wouldn't be asking for any more or any less than we're asking for.'

Michael Stewart nodded in agreement. 'You walk the streets here
and you won't find one black face serving in the shops. There's an
Aboriginal publican in the centre of town and the supermarket over
the back here employs one Aboriginal girl. But you won't see one

Aboriginal face serving in the shops. It's the same in all country towns. That's the barometer. When you see a marked presence of Aboriginal faces in some of the shops, you'll know we're on the road to reconciliation.'

The next morning, I was on the road to Wilcannia, 195 kilometres to the east. There was very little traffic and not much to see, save for a few emus. I tried preparing myself mentally for what was to come, but the truth was I had little idea what to expect. It was mid-morning when I arrived at Wilcannia and followed Smiley's directions to find Danny Rose, a consultant who is working with the community on a plan to rebuild the hospital and dramatically improve the housing. Outside the pub, a small group of men and women had gathered, waiting for the doors to open. I found Danny in a fibro house near the hospital. He was cooking a bacon and egg sandwich that would serve as breakfast and lunch. A middle-aged man in shorts, he was friendly and open, offering me a seat and a cup of instant coffee. The key plank of the plan, he explained, was to provide local employment by using 14 apprentices who had been in intensive training since July 1999.

In the warm light of day, it was easy to imagine how prosperous Wilcannia once was, with its wide streets and classic Victorian buildings, when the beautiful old shops — most of them now boarded up, faded and desolate — were open for business and the town was bustling. It once had 13 pubs. Now it has one and there is a strong minority in the town who believe the community would be better off if it went too. It stays because the local economy, sustained by welfare cheques, revolves around just two products: 'Piss and petrol', as one local put it. 'The tourists won't stop here. They buy petrol and they go. So the only businesses that make any money are the pub, the [golf] club and the service station. Everything else is either closed or closing.'

Danny took me to meet the apprentices at two of the houses they were fixing up. It didn't take me long to understand that temptation for these young men is always within earshot. Barely 80 metres away, a group of young men were opening their first VB for the day and inviting, even goading, the apprentices to join them. Six months later, their ranks were reduced to seven, but Danny Rose remained confident that these would complete their apprenticeships.

It was mid-afternoon and warm and sunny when I returned to my room in the motel that was up for sale. It wasn't, the owner stressed to me later that night, anything to do with Wilcannia being a town in decline. It was just that he and his family were ready to retire to Broken Hill. I then telephoned James Hackett at Wilcannia Central. Previously, he'd said he could not be interviewed, but was relaxed about my passing through, saying we could meet for a chat, maybe over a beer. When he rang me back, his tone had changed.

'I'm cancelling our meeting', he now said, accusing me of putting pressure on his staff to break the arrangement with '60 Minutes'. His concern was that if my story appeared before the program, they might abandon the project altogether. In short, I was jeopardising the opportunity for national television exposure of the school's achievements. I tried to reassure him, saying the only approach involved Smiley's sister, that it had not been at my instigation and that no further attempts would be made. I made no impression. Hackett hung up.

That afternoon I went to the police station and secured approval to spend the evening with Dean Whyman, one of several Aboriginal Community Liaison Officers (ACLOs) at Wilcannia, on night patrol. It is a job that involves driving around the town and its fringes, checking that all is well. Mostly, it is a taxi service for those who have had too much to drink, a service that is essential to calm fraying tempers but is also an example of people not having to take responsibility. Despite the town's reputation for violence, I saw none of it. Invariably, our passengers were inebriated but friendly, even curious about the stranger. 'Are you a lawyer?' they asked. Among them were some of the apprentices I had met earlier in the day. They spoke cheerfully about the project and the prospect of setting up their own building maintenance business when the hospital and the house projects were over.

Dean was a man of few words, but his patience made him well suited to a job which on occasions involves trying to defuse potentially violent episodes. I asked what he liked most about Wilcannia. 'I just grew up here. That's all', he said. It was as expansive as Dean became in the two nights we spent together.

I asked him what there was for young kids to do in Wilcannia and the answer was not much. Although sport is crucial in country towns like this, Wilcannia no longer fielded a football team. It hadn't for years. With one of the local sergeants, Dean was offered a coaching course at Cobar in an effort to get something happening. In the end, he chose not to take it.

A cornerstone of policing in Aboriginal communities, explained Garry Nowlan, the officer-in-charge, was discretion. 'We often take people home when they're drunk and offensive and swearing at us, rather than lock them up and put them in the cells. It can be stressful. We get referred to as "white F'ing Cs" every day of the week. We accept that. Often they'll apologise in the morning.'

But he also conceded that, too often, young and inexperienced officers had been sent to Wilcannia and places like it with little training in how to deal with people affected by substance abuse or mental illness, and no understanding of Aboriginal culture. To rectify this, he said he was planning a cultural awareness program where new police would be taken to camp out at Mutawintji, 150 kilometres away, as guests of the Barkandji people, to be told the history and shown special cultural sites. The first trip went ahead in August and was such a big success that similar trips may become mandatory training for police assigned to remote areas with significant Aboriginal populations.

The police station is a historic sandstone building and the old exercise yard of the jail makes an incongruous setting for a kind of after-hours creche. On Thursday nights, when the biggest welfare cheques come into town, children and their families are encouraged to come and sit in the yard and watch a movie on a big screen.

Sitting in his office on the second floor, Nowlan gave the impression of being pretty tough, pretty hardened. He'd spent a lot of time working in Aboriginal communities and five years in the highlands of Papua New Guinea. 'There are some good things in this community', he said. 'Most of the people in this town are good people. There's a few bad ones here, the same as any community and it's probably no more dangerous wandering the streets here at night than it would be in certain areas of Melbourne and Sydney. Basically, when trouble does erupt here it can erupt very violently and unpredictably and just as quickly disappear.' Therein lies the difference.

The next morning I drove to Bourke, a distance of around 400 kilometres, stopping at Cobar for a toasted cheese and tomato sandwich and a coffee. If there was one overall impression of what I had seen, it was that there wasn't much joy in Wilcannia. The only smiles I saw were on the faces of the children playing on the bridge above the mighty Darling River.

That day was a big day, because the Queen was visiting Bourke, accompanied by the New South Wales Premier Bob Carr and assorted other politicians and civic leaders. Compared with the stretch of highway between Wilcannia and Cobar, the traffic between Cobar and Bourke was heavy.

My aim wasn't to see the how the town greeted the Queen, but to visit Gunda Booka, the town's Community Development Employment Program (CDEP). It is a big impressive place, offering opportunities for unemployed Aborigines in arts and crafts, carpentry, metal work, horticulture and much more. But it was almost deserted when I arrived. Almost everyone was off at the park to see the Queen. But Jack Scott, the man in charge, was at his desk. A handsome man with a dry sense of humour, Scott had been doing television and radio interviews most of the morning, all of them about the Queen's coming, all of them perfunctory. Yet something inclined him to spend the next hour or so in open and sometimes urgent conversation with a stranger, as if he sensed that this might represent an opportunity to finally cut through.

The first room he showed me was where the women are taught how to make floral arrangements and wreaths. 'We have a lot of untimely deaths here, a lot of them involving our younger men, men in their mid-20s and 30s, and it seems to come in threes and fours', he explained. 'What the ladies found was that there was no place to provide affordable wreaths, so they decided to make the effort themselves. We're trying to get to the point where we can afford to bury our people with a certain amount of dignity and pride.' When Scott was a teenager, he said, 'our people died in their late 40s. Now it seems that as we're getting older, our people are dying younger. Now it's common for them to die in their 30s.' And at Enngonia, 60 kilometres north of Bourke, he said, the Aboriginal community 'are still digging their own graves with a shovel and a crowbar. They can't afford for the earth [moving] equipment to come out from Bourke to do their graves.'

The CDEP was introduced in 1976 as a work-for-the-dole program for Aboriginal communities. Gunda Booka is one of the most effective CDEPs in the country, providing employment for around 180 men and women of all ages. Aside from providing goods and services, Gunda Booka plays a crucial social role. More than a dozen teenagers who regularly came to police attention now spend time in the art and craft room, discovering talents they did not imagine they possessed.

'The program has been successful in distracting them, occupying their minds, giving them some pride, putting them back in touch with their culture', said Scott. With juvenile crime the main problem in Bourke, and lack of parental control the biggest contributing factor, the program had the potential to make a lasting impact.

Scott also planned to offer Bourke businesses a night security service and to establish a prisoner diversion hostel as an alternative to the lock-up when someone was charged. His efforts were strongly backed by Bourke's most senior policeman, Superintendent Bob McIntyre, who told me later, 'We're totally committed to support any program the community brings along to keep the young people out of the justice system'.

Scott would like to see CDEP dramatically expanded, and believed Gunda Booka could make an even bigger contribution to reconciliation in Bourke, a town that only started flying the Aboriginal flag from the Town Hall two years earlier. But he said the principle of mutual obligation that underpinned work-for-the-dole also applied to reconciliation. 'Unless the white man turns around, acknowledges his mistakes, comes clean, and then sets about genuinely and sincerely rectifying the problems, we're just going to stay as is. It's always going to be an itch that you can't scratch, a thorn in your side.'

But it wasn't only the 'whiteys' who he thought needed to lift their game. 'The whole Aboriginal community needs to take a 180 degree turn and go right back to basics. Let's look at our values, our principles, our morals, our self-esteem, who we are, our culture. It's our belief that if you haven't got a past, you haven't got a future. What the Aboriginal community needs to do at a grassroots level is re-acquaint themselves with that, re-establish that, rejuvenate it among our children. And then you've got yourself a platform from which you can work.'

The next morning I was up at five and back on the road to witness the Wilcannia Community Working Party meeting, due to begin at 9 am. In fact, it started quite some time after that, and, even then, those who were not from the community (and some who were) spent a good deal of time on the footpath outside. The experience demonstrated both the resolve of the local leadership to make things better, and the frustrations they face. In a way, it was a microcosm of the reconciliation process.

Among those present were two community elders, brothers Cyril and Ray Hunter, whose many roles include being truancy officers for the school. On a kerb opposite, a group of truants stood as a kind of brazen testimony to the difficulty of their job. One of the public servants from Broken Hill brought an old set of golf clubs to give to Ray to pass on to the kids. Giving golf lessons to the children is another of Ray's unpaid jobs.

James Hackett was a member of the working party, but he chose to send his deputy instead. Was he avoiding me? It was during the morning, in one of the conversations outside the meeting, that I first became aware of resentment in the community toward Hackett's style of leadership at the school. There was also a degree of cynicism about the forthcoming special on '60 Minutes'. There was no doubting the community's pride in Heidi's achievement, but there was a view that the school should not be taking all the credit, particularly as Heidi had completed some of her secondary schooling at Dubbo.

The first item on the agenda concerned the tenders for the new hospital. All three were well above budget and none made any undertaking to employ the local apprentices. The meeting resolved that they be asked to re-submit their bids. Progress has since been made. Key departments, particularly the Department of Community Services (DOCS) were not represented, stalling progress on a plan for a children's shelter, and there was anger that the drop-in centre's bus has been taken.

Gloria King, a community elder, made no attempt to disguise her frustration. 'It is little wonder that kids are petrol-sniffing when the town offers them so little', she said. Gloria is a Barkandji elder who was born in Wilcannia and grew up in 'an old tin shack' built by her father by the Darling River. It was 'nice and clean and tidy' and she has fond memories of sitting around the campfire, with her mother passing on the stories in the Barkandji language. She was a pre-school assistant at the mission school and ended up working there for 30 years, becoming the pre-school director. Her dream of the school becoming Aboriginal-controlled was never realised and she blames assimilation policies and welfare for the 'generation that's lost to us'.

'I don't think we've got any hope for those people, but we're trying to grab the kids, do something for them', she said. 'There's no family values or nothing like that here. We've been trying to turn that around for the last three years and we're still trying.' The elders' council was planning a meeting to discuss the situation, but Gloria said the options were limited.

Evelyn Barker, another member of the working party who ran the women's safehouse, was similarly concerned about the young. As we stood talking after the meeting she told me how important it was for kids to know where they come from and have pride in their identity. Then she added earnestly, 'But they're quite confused and angry, and it's the anger that frightens me, 'cause I'm 50 and I think that we had a bit, but we didn't have as much as is here today'.

The school had a request to expand its nutrition program so that students had access to three healthy meals a day. The relevant agency wasn't present but the meeting endorsed the idea in principle. The discussion underscored the dilemma facing many indigenous communities: if they feed the children, they will only further entrench the hand-out mentality and encourage parents to abdicate their responsibilities; if they let them go hungry, the children will be even less likely to attend school, much less digest their lessons.

One of the interruptions was when the chair of the working party, William Bates, was called outside, apparently by James Hackett. When Bates came back into the room, he called me out. Hackett had come for some other reason, he indicated, but had also told Bates he should be aware that I had written a particularly negative piece about the Queen's visit to Bourke. He didn't have a copy of it. Bates accepted my word that I had not written anything from Bourke, positive or negative, and we went back inside.

Then there was a request from the local council for a big effort to make the town look its best when '60 Minutes' came to town. The idea was supported, but Gloria King reminded those present that the council had not been so enthusiastic on Clean Up Australia Day. 'That was a most disappointing day for me', she said. Her point was taken, but the idea was adopted. As Bates wryly put it: 'If Bourke can do it for the Queen, we can do it for "60 Minutes"'.

That night I struck up a conversation with an old woman and accompanied her as she walked several of her grandchildren to their respective homes. One refused to be dropped off and sat crying in the middle of an intersection. 'Go home to your mother!' his grandmother called, feigning sternness. 'Why won't he go?' I asked. 'Because his father's drinking.' Her tone was flat, matter-of-fact, unemotional. By the time I had walked her and two other grandchildren to her own door, the crying boy is hovering outside, having run the other way around the block to test her will-power once more. She relented and beckoned him inside, in what I suspected was a familiar occurence.

From the scrub across the road, you could hear strange, wild sounds. What were they? 'The petrol sniffers', the old woman said. I discovered later that their regular rituals posed a challenge for both the police and the ACLOs. Neither had an answer to the problem. Gary Nowlan explained that some children, from six to 26 years old, sniffed petrol every day. 'Kids are breaking into the service station bowsers at night, draining out the dregs of petrol from the bowser hoses, wandering the streets sniffing petrol from Coke bottles all night', he said 'What makes it worse is there's no offence. All we can do is take them home and give them to their parents. Half the time, they beat us back down the street and they're doing it again.' He thought petrol sniffing was a health issue, not a police issue. 'But the health authorities don't know how to deal with it, the Aboriginal community don't know how to deal with it, the Education Department don't know and we're in a similar dilemma. If anybody else has got any ideas, we'd love to hear from them.'

The other problem that was dividing the community, indeed the root of many of its problems (including the petrol sniffing), was grog. Although voluntary controls on the sale of full-strength beer had resulted in a dramatic fall in assaults, there was a push to revert to open slather. Nowlan was preparing to defend the restrictions with the state liquor administration board.

Before leaving town the next morning, after another couple of uneventful hours in the van with Dean Whyman, I visited St Therese's Community School, which offers places from kindergarten to Year Two, where Weet-bix were being served to the students as a once-a-week treat. On other days there is milk, a piece of fruit at recess and sandwiches for lunch. Sister Margaret McGrath had been principal there for seven years and disagreed with the Central School's policy of providing full meals. 'I tell the teachers we are not here to fill them up. That's their parents' responsibility.' The key to making progress, she believed, was to get the parents well. The key to that was boosting employment.

Were things improving? 'You make advances, then you take steps back and then you go through deep valleys. If I was just here to see results, I don't think I'd be here.'

Then there were two more stops. I called by the hospital, where Heidi was then one of five health trainees, to meet her and offer congratulations on her achievement. We spoke briefly about the importance of role models and I left. Then I called in on the Central School to tell James Hackett there were no hard feelings and to wish him well with '60 Minutes'. He kept me waiting long enough for me to consider leaving. Then he sent the deputy principal out with a blunt message: I was banned from the school grounds and should leave immediately. Then she was gone.

My series of articles was published a few weeks later in *The Age*, beginning on Saturday 20 May. As fate had it, Ray Martin's report went to air on '60 Minutes' the following evening. It was called 'A Class of their Own' and it concentrated on the school and three teachers who were 'trying to save a generation of children'. They were dubbed the three musketeers. Midway through the program, Martin delivered a monologue, saying, 'Spend a bit of time here, and you learn that the school gives some children what they don't get at home. It gives them food, love but most of all it gives them safety. In

19

small country towns people don't like to talk publicly, but privately those who know will tell you shocking stories about violence and about abuse, especially abuse against young girls.'

This was followed by an interview with James Hackett and a quote almost identical to the one Martin had used in his column about Heidi Bugmy, leaving no doubt about the original source. Said the principal: 'I guess if a girl growing up in Wilcannia can make it to 18 and not be pregnant or have a child or two already, to not have been a victim of domestic violence or interference, [that's] very rare and I'd say a special person'.

Martin replied, 'That's remarkable isn't it? For most Canadians, for most Australians, to hear someone who knows say for a girl to reach 18 and not be pregnant and not be bashed up is a rarity is a shocking indictment.'

Hackett continued, 'The police, they tell me that almost all of our children are interfered with'.

Almost all? It was hard to imagine a statement more likely to provoke a hostile reactions from those who must be part of the equation if lasting improvements are to be made. Yet the allegation was not put to either parents or the police in the program. It went uncontested. Was it the truth? Not according to those, like Garry Nowlan, who told me domestic violence and child neglect and abuse were serious problems in places like Wilcannia, but not to the extent asserted by Hackett.

There was more in the program on the prevalence of violence and the claim that half the students would go hungry if they were not fed at school. The deputy principal told how female students confided that their boyfriends did not love them unless they bashed them. Alison Johnson expressed a view I would hear again and again in places like Cape York and Katherine, from people like Noel Pearson — that passive welfare was the cause of much of Wilcannia's problems. She also supported the closing of the pub, a sentiment later endorsed by Gloria King.

Given the build-up within the town, including the clean-up project, over many weeks to the 'good news' story '60 Minutes' was expected to tell, it was not surprising that the town reacted badly. Many parents took their children out of the school. Their anger prompted a '60 Minutes' crew to return to cover an angry meeting.

Martin reported the following week that three of the girls he had interviewed had been bashed since the report had aired. One of the three, he said, had attempted suicide. Another had both her arms broken with an iron bar. This was denied by people in the town, who maintained the bashings and attempted suicide were unrelated to the allegations aired on the program and took place before '60 Minutes' came to town. Nowlan later confirmed this to be true. No-one challenged Martin's conclusion that 'what began as a positive story about Wilcannia Central School's triumph had ended with angry parents, empty classrooms and shattered teachers'.

Alison Johnson left Wilcannia the week the '60 Minutes' story went to air. The deputy principal followed, and James Hackett, who had tried so hard to make a difference in a hurry, was gone without warning in October. 'We saw the removal van truck pull up and he was gone', said one local. 'No good-byes. No explanations.'

Months later I finally did speak to Alison Johnson, Smiley's sister. She recalled how she cried all the way to Griffith after leaving the town, how there were days when she still yearned for the sight of the great Darling River. She had gone back over the program a million times in her mind, she said, and she thought there were things that could have been said more subtly, and people who had reason to feel unfairly maligned. But she did not regret one word she uttered. In the end, she explained, she had to decide whether she was a professional teacher speaking what she knew to be true, or a member of a community who had grown up in an environment of passive welfare and all its attendant social problems. It was, she said, a case of 'beat 'em, or join 'em', of having to make a choice between challenging the status quo or defending it.

'I'm a single mum. I've got a little seven and eight-year-old and I don't care what it takes. I don't expect DOCS, I don't expect the Government, I don't expect Joe Blow down the road to be accountable for my kids. At the end of the day when they come home, I'm there for them and I'm encouraging them with their homework. Is that so hard? Is that wrong?'

And what of the allegations about the extent of family violence, sexual interference and abuse? Johnson had no doubt that they too could have been expressed better, but she was just as adamant that these issues had to be addressed honestly and openly for the sake of the children. 'Somewhere along the line, who's going to speak up for those kids who are being abused? Who's going to speak up?' She regretted the loss of friendships, 'and the sadness that was caused all around', and she wanted to apologise to the people who were 'tarred and feathered'. 'But on the other hand, the reality is that things are happening and somebody's got speak up. We can pretend, but if you're a person living in that community, you've got to be honest.'

After-school tranquility at Challenger Bay, showing the idyllic side of Palm Island.

Michael Gordon

2 Palm Island: A paradise denied

It's just sad that the first thing that came into the hands of our people was the pub and the drink. Dulcie Isaro

We know the things that aren't taught in schools, 'cos the old people told us. Robert Blackley

He seemed a decent bloke, not least because he took pity on me on a hot day in Townsville. Outside the airport, I asked him where the flights departed for Palm Island. 'Throw your bag in the back', he said. 'I'll give you a lift.'

He also gave me a free analysis of 'Palm', the could-be paradise that achieved international notoriety when the 1999 edition of *The Guinness Book of Records* sensationally (and wrongly) dubbed it the most violent place on earth outside a combat zone. From a man who had worked on the island's airstrip, the analysis boiled down to a single sentence: what the blackfellas had done to Palm was an 'absolute tragedy'.

What I didn't fully appreciate at the time was just what Palm Island had done to the blackfellas. Dulcie Isaro was the first person to set me straight. She was 15 when her father was arrested at 4 am in 1957 and marched at gunpoint and in leg irons to a waiting RAAF patrol boat.

And why? Because her father, Willie Thaiday, was one of the seven men who led a demonstration against the £2 per-week wages paid to Palm Island workers and the practice of docking their pay packets for no good reason. A machine gun was trained on the prisoners until daybreak, when their wives and children were given the choice of going with them to the mainland. All the while, the group confounded their captors by raucously singing what Willie called 'an island song about our home'.

Willie had ten children, the youngest four months, and one grandchild. They all went with him and spent a week in the watchhouse cells at Townsville on the way to Woorabinda. It was a tough trip and Willie remarked later that they were jammed up like fish in a tin. With him was one of the other leaders of the strike, Sonny Sibley, the great-uncle of Cathy Freeman. Freeman's maternal grandmother, Alice Sibley, who was taken from her family near Cooktown when she was eight years old and sent to Palm, and her daughter (Cathy's mother), Cecelia, followed five days later.

I met Willie Thaiday's daughter at the Palm Island Aboriginal Council office soon after I arrived. We spoke on a deck outside the office, overlooking a reserve named Freedom Park in honour of the rebels. Dulcie Isario described the episode as 'the best thing that ever happened on Palm Island'. She has written her own account of it and hopes that it will be used in the local school to teach children their history.

Her father's story, told orally, was published in 1981, the first book in Australia to be solely produced by Aboriginal people. It was called *Under The Act*. Barely 50 pages, the book is one man's testimony to the inhumanity that was Palm Island, the place that became known as a penal colony for 'troublesome Aborigines' after is was established in 1918. Yet his story is told without malice and with a hint of optimism. As Dulcie said, 'My father used to say, "What we're suffering now, future generations will benefit from". It's just sad that the first thing that came into the hands of our people was the pub and the drink.'

The 'Act' of the book's title was the Queensland legislation that then governed that state's Aboriginal peoples. Until the 1967 referendum, the states had the sole power to make such laws. The referendum proposal was to remove the discrimination against Aboriginal people in the Constitution by giving the Commonwealth the power to make laws for Aborigines and Torres Strait Islanders, and to include them in the count of Australia's population. It did not give Aborigines and Torres Strait Islanders the vote, as this was legislated for federal elections in 1962 (Queensland was the last state government to provide indigenous enfranchisement, in 1965), but it offered the hope that Aborigines would be removed from the often discriminatory state legislation and administration.

The referendum gained the highest 'yes' vote of any question put to the people since Federation, with almost 90 per cent of voters in support. Sadly, it did little to change the material or emotional condition of indigenous people. In an editorial published three months later, on 3 August 1967, *The Age* lamented the failure of the government led by Harold Holt to give the slightest hint of what it intended to do with its new power. Expressing sentiments that could also apply to much of the official response to indigenous issues before and since, the paper complained that the Federal Government had responded as if the vote had been overwhelmingly 'no'. 'The Government cannot excuse its silence and inaction by pretending that the problem must be looked at for a long time before it can be tackled', it said, adding:

> The problem is painfully clear, and some of the remedies are obvious and easy to apply ... Money alone will not produce tolerance and mutual respect between black and white, but in today's harsh world it is essential equipment on the march towards these qualities.

It took until the arrival of the Whitlam Government in 1972 for things to begin to change in most Aboriginal communities, including Palm Island.

The whites-only school had just closed in 1972 when Bill Blackley, a wide-eyed 19-year-old teacher, arrived from Brisbane. At the time, the majority of homes had no refrigerators and the only store routinely had no milk or fresh foods. 'When I came here it was really strange', Blackley told me, 'You'd walk along the street and all the old gentlemen would tip their hat, and I thought, "What courteous people". Then I found out that before the referendum, they got 14 days jail if they didn't tip their hat.'

Two years after he arrived, Blackley married Maggie, the Aboriginal school secretary. They have six children and now, after a period away, live out of town on a secluded beach and run the only alternative to the government-owned store. It carries the scars of more break-ins than Blackley would care to remember.

Blackley was among those who attended the public meeting in 1972 that decided to open a pub. 'All the women had come down and when they asked for a show of hands, they all voted against the proposal', he says. 'The vote was carried, but I'm absolutely convinced to this day that if they'd done a count, it wouldn't have got through.' Something else happened after 1972. 'When I came here there was no dole. You could not get an unemployment benefit on the Palm. Shortly thereafter, it changed.'

For half-a-century the Aborigines on Palm Island lived under a virtual dictatorship. The superintendent decided whether they could marry, severely punished those who practised their culture, denied

25

them access to alcohol, separated children from parents and rewarded hard work with inadequate rations. It was not uncommon for those who bucked the system to have their heads shaved and be imprisoned. Then, when freedom was finally given, they were left without the tools to capitalise on it. As Ernest Hunter, a psychiatrist who has worked in remote Aboriginal Australia for 15 years, says: 'Suddenly, they had access to the dreams of the mainstream, but the sense of exclusion was more pronounced'. So began what Hunter has called the period of deregulation on Aboriginal communities — and its unintended consequences.

'I remember a South African saying to me, "You know, you've been far more successful in apartheid here in Australia than we ever were in South Africa". And he's absolutely correct', Hunter says. 'Because the result is that people on remote communities, whether they want to leave or not, can't because they can't survive outside.'

The immediate dividend was an upsurge in violence, particularly on Palm, where eight women were murdered in one year. But more than two decades on, the legacy is far more complex, the problems far more intractable. Twenty years ago suicide was unheard of in indigenous communities. So was diabetes. Now both are endemic. John Howard might call this a black armband view of the present, but it goes a long way to explain Palm Island today: a place of jarring contrasts between natural beauty and the remnants of authoritarianism, of sporting talent and wasted potential, of disarming honesty and deep-seated hostility.

I experienced all these things in the space of two hours, walking alone between the council office and the cemetery, maybe four kilometres apart along a coastal road. First, I stopped by the old hall, where Ray Dennis, a quietly spoken white man, was coaching children on how to box. He recently took five of them to the national championships and came away with three firsts and two seconds. 'I'd rather live here than the mainland', he told me. 'It's a lot safer for me walking around here than the main street in Townsville — and these people here, they all respect me, the drunks, everyone. Everyone speaks to me. I don't think I've had more friends in my life than what I've got here.' He then produced a couple of newspaper clippings from his pocket on the achievements of his boys, before turning his attention back to the three awaiting his instructions.

Then I walked down to the jetty, where a big group of children who had just finished school were swimming. I produced my camera and several of them enjoyed playing up to it. There was one boy in particular, perched high on a pole in the water that seemed impossible to climb. He stayed there while I photographed him and then he dived into the water several metres below.

Then I passed the compound where the police, teachers and hospital staff live removed from the general population behind a high barbed-wire fence. While the formal segregation of blacks and whites ended almost three decades ago, the separation between those who lived inside and outside the compound seemed just as absolute.

Further on, I witnessed a bitter domestic argument that spilled onto the street, an obviously drunk woman taunting a man with every obscenity you can imagine. But he refused to be provoked.

Before a perfect sunset, I skimmed stones across Challenger Bay with a group of young boys, then passed dozens of people who seemed to be living utterly functional lives: tending their gardens, mowing the lawn, sipping tea. Then, on an almost deserted stretch, I came across a young man walking in the opposite direction. When he was within five metres, he shouted at the top of his voice: 'You fucking black cunt!' It was a second or two before I realised he was addressing someone else, someone well down the road, and that he hadn't even noticed I was there. When he did see me, he displayed what Henry Reynolds has called an 'all-embracing, inherited sense of forced subordination'. He almost cowered as he apologised. 'No worries', I muttered, and walked on.

But my most disturbing experience was the cemetery itself and the preponderance of crosses for those who died as children or before they reached 40. Among them were three who had committed suicide and one who was murdered, all four deaths in the four months since New Year's Eve. Bill Blackley told me later that 1300 people had died on Palm Island since he arrived in 1972. If these people had enjoyed the life expectancy of the Australian population, 70 per cent of them would still be alive. 'It's a tragedy of unspeakable proportion', he said.

It was almost dark when I returned to my modest motel room, where a sign on the wall reminded me that this is not a place for tourists: it warns that heavy equipment must be left outside. I passed by the police station that is built more like a fortress. Children were playing a game of cat and mouse, throwing rocks at the door and then running away when the police emerged to vent their anger. The night was balmy and it was tempting to venture out past the barbed-wire fence that protects the motel, but I opted for caution. My evening meal was two packets of potato chips washed down by orange juice bought from the government-owned store before it closed at 4.30 pm.

That night I started a routine that would continue for the remainder of the journey. I reviewed the day's interviews on my tape recorder and transcribed them longhand, jotting down my overall impressions. Originally, I thought the best way to approach this assignment would be to tackle one issue in each place I visited. It might have been employment in Wilcannia, or history's legacy in Palm Island, or health in Cape York, or juvenile justice in the Northern Territory. But when I confided this strategy to a woman in Cairns, she dismissed it as a whitefella's approach. Just tell the story of what happens on your trip, she told me. The issues would soon become clear enough. So that is what I did. Each morning, I would set out wearing those cargo shorts with enough pockets to carry my camera, tape recorder, notebook and blockout and still have both hands free. Each evening, I reviewed what I had seen and heard. Compared with the more familiar journalist's world of phones, fax machines, computers screens and media events, it was a liberating experience. At the back of one of the notebooks I kept a list, based on my interviews, of signposts to a reconciled Australia. It would happen, according to the list, when:

- There were black faces serving behind the counters in country towns.
- There were coffee shops and laundromats in Aboriginal communities.
- Black and white kids sat next to each other in class, and played at each other's houses after school.
- The proportion of young people buried in the cemeteries in black communities was the same as the broader population.
- White Australia took the initiative in learning about black culture.
- Black people were happy.

The second day on Palm Island, I spent mainly with Robert Blackley, one of Bill's sons. He was soon to be elected chairman of the Palm Island Aboriginal Council, at 24 becoming the youngest person to hold the top job in an Aboriginal community. I had met Robert at the council the previous day and been struck by his casual demeanour, his healthy disrespect for the way things were, and his desire to bring about change.

We set off in a four-wheel drive to tour the remote corners of the island, where families had gone to live without amenities, just to be away from the impact of grog. But heavy rains had made even the four-wheel drive tracks impassable and we were forced to turn back. The consolation was a cup of coffee at the Blackley home and a stroll along their pristine beach.

At the time, Robert's future was uncertain. He was one of three people vying for the last two places on the nine-member council. Even then, he was quietly confident that the last postal votes would see him elected and that his more senior colleagues would elect him as their chairman. When this was confirmed a week or so later, his father congratulated him with the words 'I'm very pleased you're captain of the ship. I'm just not sure whether it's the *Titanic* or the *Bounty*'.

The prime minister may have an open timetable on reconciliation, but Blackley was a young man in a hurry. 'I want to turn this place around and then head off to Canberra and change the policy at a macro-level', he said. 'We've got to be inside to change things, but we're not going to do it if we're not elected. I feel obligated to work for the people because I know I've got the knowledge, the skill and the drive and energy to do it.'

While the idea of designated seats for indigenous people in parliament was canvassed in the Council for Reconciliation's draft strategy on indigenous rights, Blackley had his eye is on winning Labor endorsement for a Senate seat. 'Quota systems are crap tokenism', he said. 'I don't want to be the token murri [Aborigine]. I've been the token black for too long. I'm still the token black on a number of committees. I'd support political parties targeting safe seats for indigenous people.'

For the next few years, however, Blackley faced multiple challenges trying to improve things on Palm. There was a vision plan to implement, which included developing employment that 'suits the island', like aquaculture and eco-tourism. And there were the problems of suicide, violence, sexual abuse, teenage pregnancy, alcohol and an emerging drug problem that had to be tackled on multiple fronts on a daily basis. Part of the solution was to replace what Blackley called the '"real" Aboriginal industry'. This was a reference to the phrase John Howard had used to attack indigenous critics of his Aboriginal affairs minister, John Herron, in July of 1996. It was also the phrase Pauline Hanson used in her maiden speech on 11 September 1996 in vitriolic condemnation of the taxpayer-funded 'industry' that serviced Aboriginal people, an industry she saw as including members of the Council for Aboriginal Reconciliation. The 'real' Aboriginal industry, said Blackley, was the 40 or so white public servants and contractors who flew in and out of Palm Island each weekday, many of them utterly detached from the community. His ambition was to equip the local population to perform these tasks. Ultimately, Blackley dreamed of Palm Island being the sort of place middle-class Aborigines from the cities might want to retire.

One of the reasons Blackley was well placed to make a contribution is that he knows the history of the island and has lived it. He had also been educated off the island, gone to boarding school in Charters Towers and spent some time at university, although without finishing his degree.

'It's just atrocious what happened. We know the things that aren't taught in schools, 'cos the old people told us. Most of the people sent here were light-skinned, like my great grandmother. Governed by the bell, under the thumb. My mum had to stand up in line as a child to receive a bit of flour, bit of sugar, bit of teas, fat on bones to take home to feed the whole family. That's my mum. She's 47. It's not a long time ago. She was still picking up rations when she was 18. I find it unforgivable. The things they did to my nana was worse. The Health Department, what they did to the little girls on Palm. It's sickening.'

The thing about the violence, he said later, was that it involves people who loved each other. 'Cousins hurting cousins. Sisters hurting sisters. Wives stabbing husbands.'

Much of the darker side of the history of this place of extraordinary natural beauty is passed on orally to new generations by those who have lived there. Much is also documented on the public record, like the story of Fantome, one of the islands in the Palm group. Before becoming a leprosarium for Aborigines in 1940, Fantome was a 'lock' hospital (for the treatment of venereal diseases). In 1932, the head of the Australian Institute of Tropical Medicine, Dr Raphael Cilento, outlined this vision for the island:

> The whole abo population should be worked through Fantome and then re-graded into new cases, incurable aged, incurable young and part-cured and thence drafted when clean back into Palm from which they can be sent out into the mainland to be (1) assimilated if white enough; (2) employed under supervision and protection; or (3) kept on Palm.

The scale of the task facing Blackley was underscored when

I obtained a copy of a confidential report on Palm Island and Doomadgee by a team led by Australia's most senior Aboriginal policeman, Colin Dillon, handed to the Federal Government in April, one month before my arrival. The report summarised the problems under a series of headings. Here are a few edited examples:

Substance abuse: The degree of alcohol and drug abuse was a concern raised by virtually every person consulted. Many considered that the substance abuse problems in these communities were a direct result of the lack of employment and social opportunities and the complex and often traumatic history of communities ... In the case of Palm Island, the community's reliance on the profits from the tavern has created a vicious cycle of dependence on the proceeds from alcohol sales to fund essential community projects. In the case of Doomadgee, the considerable amount of money spent on alcohol at the 'Hells gate' roadhouse and the Burketown Hotel every pay day continues to drain the community of much needed funds.

Law and order: One of the alarming issues to come out of the visit was the degree of social disorder in each of the communities. The review team was particularly concerned to learn that many of the youth in these communities had very little parental supervision or indeed guidance. In addition, the rate of violent crimes is alarming and reports of rape, domestic violence, sexual physical abuse and assaults are at critical point.

Education: Both communities have difficulty encouraging children to attend school. The serious problems in the family household and in the wider community, the lack of parental skills and the lack of employment and training opportunities (leading to a lack of personal goals) have a negative impact on students.

Counselling services: Many of the residents, including children, have been subjected to physical and mental abuse and have witnessed violent crimes such as murder, serious assault and rape. Many had attempted or witnessed suicide or had suffered from dislocation in their families. The lack of counselling services was seen as a major problem in these communities.

Cost of living: The price of goods (in many cases double that of mainstream stores) and the poor quality of goods did little to encourage healthy living habits.

Dillon said he had come to the view that many of the problems besetting the communities were 'a manifestation of past injustices and the impact of laws and policies enacted by governments and church administrations in an attempt to control the lives of the people of these communities'. The rebuilding process, he said, required a renewed recognition of the rights of residents. There was also a need for major reform in the service delivery approach of government and substantial change at a community level to empower residents.

Over my three days on the island, I probably spoke to many of those who had participated in Dillon's study, and I came away with many of the same conclusions. A health worker who asked not to be

31

identified highlighted the difficulties in working in a community where it is rare for people to live beyond 50, where sexual health remains a big problem, where teenage pregnancy is accepted as the norm, where cardio-vascular disease and diabetes are serious problems, where there are domestic violence incidents requiring hospital attention four or five times a week, and where it is impossible to pay anything like adequate attention to prevention. 'Do we go from day to day putting Bandaids on? Yes. Do we have a plan to do better? Yes. Do we have the resources to implement it? No.' A youth worker who also sought anonymity lamented that too many projects started without planning or money, only to be terminated. 'Some very positive things are happening, but too slowly and certainly not enough and maybe too late.'

Responsibility for helping victims of family violence and tackling the problem fell heavily — too heavily — on the women's centre, which was established in 1985 after the eight murders. It is situated in a small building and was run by Selena Solomon and Delena Foster, both of them victims of domestic violence. Delena was on call 24 hours a day, servicing a community of at least 1000 women without the back-up of a women's shelter. Aside from Selena, there were two men's support workers on limited hours, but both were at TAFE improving their literacy and numeracy skills when I visited.

Reconciliation between indigenous and non-indigenous Australians is not a subject often discussed on Palm Island, but Delena was among those who believed reconciliation within the Aboriginal community, made up of people drawn from more than 40 tribes, was an essential first step. As Sylvia Reubin, the woman who gave me a lift from the airport put it: 'We are the youngest tribe in the Aboriginal nation, made by the white man's pen. So we've got to reconcile amongst ourselves.'

Perhaps the biggest positive is what Delena describes as a willingness to begin to face up to the problems. 'There's been a lot of abuse. I worked for child care for about four years and the amount of sexual abuse, physical abuse, emotional abuse and neglect that happens that was all hush hush — nobody wanted to talk about it. And incest. But now it's sort of coming out and people are being more aware of it. People were coming up to me and talking about it and wanting something done.' She thought that they had to target the young people, and involve the men's support worker. 'We have some good role models in the community who are responsible fathers. Get them to talk to the young people. We did a survey and a lot of men said they don't want to hit their women but at that moment they can't control their anger, that's it's the only way they know because they've been brought up in violent situations. We've got to break that cycle. I know it's going to be a lot of work, that nothing is going to change overnight. We've got to target those young men and women coming up from school and let them know that violence is not the answer.'

Delena's analysis was consistent with the main conclusion of a report on violence written for the Apunipima Cape York Health Council by Geoff Genever. He wrote:

> Until Aboriginal people, particularly young men, recognise that aspects of their behaviour are maiming their society and killing their people just as bullets and arsenic once did, communities will continue to be physically and intellectually impoverished by the absence of so many of their number who spend some of their most productive years behind bars. Their women will continue to live in a state of terror and their children will be exposed to influences that will perpetuate the situation.

The problem is much the same as the one '60 Minutes' highlighted at Wilcannia, but the way of dealing with it appears to represent a striking contrast. The message from the '60 Minutes' program was that nearly all virtue resided inside the school and that progress was being made in spite of the community. It was not a fair representation, for one of James Hackett's benchmarks for success was parental participation in school activities. The result in Wilcannia was to set back the community several years. On Palm, the problems were of a similar magnitude, if not greater, but the strategy was at least clearly understood: engage the community, target the young, recognise role models. Empower them. Applaud them.

Robert Blackley believed one of the biggest underlying problems was that people have nothing to look forward to, no feasts, not even famines. Nothing to celebrate. This, he hoped, was changing. After ten years of trying, there was optimism that a Palm Island rugby league team would be admitted into the Townsville and district competition in 2001. Coinciding with the Olympics, the island's first cultural festival was staged over three days in September. There were local bands, speeches, marches and a star attraction who performed each night on television. Her name was Cathy Freeman.

Michael Gordon

Kuka Yalanji elders Peter Fischer and
George Kulka at Buru, an outstation that
could be a model for Cape York communities.

3 Cape York: Looking for a laundromat

There's no leadership model for where we're going, only a multitude of possibilities, and I'm going to try my hand at the hardest and push for the one I think we deserve. Kerry Arabena, Cape York Health Council

They grabbed him, took him to Yarrabah Mission. He cried his guts out and after two months he died. We was about five years old, a half-caste kid. Peter Fischer, Buru (China Camp)

The sticks and stones of racism are wounds that you suffer externally. The whole welfare thing is viral. It actually gets inside you and breaks you down from the inside — and that's what it's done in Aboriginal society. Noel Pearson, Cairns

I arrived at Cairns around midday on a Wednesday, ready for the transition from the Palm Island Motel to the Cairns Hilton — and keen to find a laundromat. Alastair Harris, who was working with the Apunipima Cape York Health Council at the time, had other ideas. Weeks earlier, over the phone, he had offered to take me to visit some Aboriginal communities on the Cape and maybe an out-station, too. Now, he kindly met me at the airport and suggested we best head off that night. There was much to do.

Before we left, he took me to meet Apunipima's director, a tall striking woman with a big smile and an even bigger capacity for plain-speaking, Kerry Arabena. We were introduced at the office and soon adjourned to a bar near the Cairns Art Gallery. Over coffee and cake, Arabena spoke with disarming candor about the challenges on Cape York, her hopes for the partnership plan being promoted by Noel Pearson, and the physical and mental toll that advocacy of change can take on those willing to take leadership roles. 'I just thank heaven I'm six foot sometimes', she said.

A woman well skilled in the art of extracting more out of less, she condensed her own life story to a single paragraph, explaining

35

that while her Aboriginality came from the Torres Strait, she had always felt more culturally comfortable in the desert. 'I was born in Brisbane in 1968, went to school and uni there and went running off to the desert as soon as I could. I had my son when I was 19 and my daughter when I was 23, did a social work degree, went off and worked in welfare for a year and then went running out bush with a mob that only walked out of the desert in the 1960s. I sat out with the Pintubi fellas and ran their health service for them. Then I came back into Alice and moved back to Cairns because my grandmother was up here at the time. She's from Murray Island up on the Torres Strait.'

One of the fundamental aims of the partnership plan, she explained, was to frame strategies for communities based on their assets, rather than concentrate on the problems. 'We know our problems inside out', she said. 'What we have now is a whole lot of infrastructure in communities that is problem-orientated. For family violence, we have women's shelters. For drug and alcohol problems, we've got local lock-ups. But we don't have anything normalised in our communities. There are no coffee shops. No laundromats.'

Arabena saw her investment in the partnership plan as 'normalising' community infrastructure, 'so if I want to go to a chemist to buy something, I don't have to go to the hospital to see a nurse, a doctor, to get a pharmacy slip'. That is a ridiculous waste of health resources. 'We've got all the health resources we need. It's just a matter of making sure that they operate more effectively and we normalise people's interactions with them.'

In the world Arabena would like to see, the health performance indicators would not be just about how many people come through the clinic for a particular chronic disease, but how many contacts the diabetes educator had with those who were vulnerable to the disease. 'These people are just not around at the moment', she said. While diabetes and other chronic diseases cause enormous distress, the problem as she sees it is that sufferers may not come into contact with the health system until they need renal dialysis, 'which is way too late. There have been various points in that person's life where there could have been very effective intervention, and what we want to focus on is looking at all of the upstream issues around health, not just a service that deals with ill-health. All we want is what every other Australian both expects and takes for granted.'

Perhaps the biggest challenge is to confront the problem of

alcohol, but Arabena was convinced it is something that cannot be done head-on. 'There's a range of different things you've got to do to fill in people's days.' She thought the people on the communities were 'just extraordinary' because 'they wake up every morning and they can look their life down the barrel of a gun. They know what they're going to be doing, day in, day out. They get excited about watching "Bold and Beautiful" at 4 o'clock in the afternoon because, quite frankly, there are limited choices. There are a number of things that impact: overcrowded, close-up housing, not being able to complete education, no jobs if you get education. So grog's the easy option.'

Arabena said she had heard the most inane stories from black people about the grog. One was that they would get sick *with the detox* if the grog was taken away; or that they *deserved* to spend their welfare cheques on whatever they wished because this is compensation for their dispossession. 'Stupid, stupid stories', said Arabena.

'What it's about is having your life filled with meaningful choices which make you happy — and I have not met very many happy Aboriginal or Islander people living in their communities. The impact of the traumas of the last couple of generations is enormous. So is the impact of government policies which set out to denigrate people and to minimise their existence. So the minimalist existence that many people choose is to be an alcoholic and not to take responsibility.'

The challenge for leaders and communities, she said, was to stop talking about being marginalised and *dis*-advantaged, and start talking about success and advantage. 'I'm sick of having to denigrate people's efforts in communities in order to get funds for projects. I want to be able to go into my communities and say "You are doing really well, look at all the assets you have, let's find ways of building them up". Let's take the "dis" out of it.'

Arabena thought that turning this around would require 'remoralising' entire communities. 'We have to ask ourselves: Is it all right to go flogging up your partner? Is it all right for 12-year-old girls to get pregnant? We have to remoralise our society, and ensure that there is some discipline when people step out of line. We have to start punishing bad behaviour and rewarding good behaviour.'

We spoke about reconciliation and Arabena's firm view was that choices were not only facing black Australia. 'I'm hoping people look beyond what's happening today to when their grandchildren or great grandchildren will be adults and having to live with what we leave them', she said. 'People see all this indigenous stuff as problematic, that we're problem people who belong to problem communities, who have disadvantaged themselves because they jump up and down and scream from the sidelines. Well, the fact is that that's the only place we've been able to occupy, the sidelines.'

She thought that was changing. 'Now, a few of us have gone through the education systems, we've learnt bureaucratic process, we've become extraordinarily competent and still been able to maintain ties back to our communities. But the balance is extraordinary and that's what it's like to be black in this society. You never have to question whether the playing field is level. You take it for granted [that it's not] and make assumptions about it every day. Indigenous leaders in this country are bloody exhausted by the time they get to the starting line and then we've got the race to run. And some of us are tired. And some of us give up. And there are others who consistently and legitimately keep putting these views across. Those people are my heroes.' Arabena had tears in her eyes as she named some of them: people like Noel Pearson, like Pat and Michael Dodson, like Marcia Langton and Barbara Flick.

As for herself, Arabena said she had positioned herself on the bottom rung of a very interesting ladder. 'There's no leadership model for where we're going, only a multitude of possibilities, and I'm going to try my hand at the hardest and push for the one I think we deserve', she said. 'I've got a very strong, very clear agenda about what I want to see happen and I'll drag people kicking and screaming some of the way towards it and then they'll recognise, "Hey, this isn't so bad and, yes, we can have a win-win situation". When that's happened, I'll know I've done a really good job.'

It is measure of the energy expended, and maybe the magnitude of the task, that when I spoke to Kerry Arabena by telephone six months later, she had made a tactical retreat. Her commitment to the objectives she outlined with such passion and conviction when we met over coffee was undiminished, but she had handed over the reins of the health council to Doreen Hart, a Cape York woman. The change, she believed, would give the partnership plan more credibility in the communities, and more chance of winning their support. It would also allow her to focus on other priorities, particularly improving sexual health in indigenous communities. The key she said, was to build a sense of self-respect among men and women. Achieve that, and many of the other objectives would be within reach.

That night I went shopping with Alastair Harris at a Cairns supermarket for some provisions. Then we headed up to Cape Tribulation, arriving at the Daintree River ferry before dark. He gave me some insights into the Aboriginal personalities on the Cape and some background on the people I would meet, before we started talking music and discovered our mutual regard for Neil Young. We spent the night in some roadside cabins and completed the trip to Wujal Wujal the following morning. Although we didn't have far to travel, progress was slow. Several creeks were almost impassable and, at one point, we had to turn back and borrow a saw from a backpackers' hostel to clear a fallen tree that was blocking the dirt road.

Wujal Wujal, formerly the Bloomfield River Lutheran Mission, is a community of a few hundred people. It is nestled into some beautiful hilly country near the Wujal Wujal Falls, a site of special significance to the local population. In the wet season, the road south can be cut for weeks at a time, making contact with the world outside problematic. Although this is designated a 'dry' community, alcohol is readily available from outlets like 'The Den', some 20 kilometres (but an hour's drive) to the north. Thursday is when the women's welfare cheques come in. 'Pay day' for the rest of the community is Friday. The danger period for domestic violence lasts until Saturday, when the money inevitably dries up.

Doreen Jones, an aunt of Noel Pearson, is the community's life promotion officer, a job that is as much about dealing with grief as it is about preventing suicides. Last year, the community lost two of its young men, including a son of Peter Wallace, who had just been elected to lead the Aboriginal council. Doreen was sitting at a table in the community hall when we arrived. In the house next door, a group of maybe a dozen people was playing cards, some of them drinking. It wasn't yet midday.

It is not uncommon here, or in other communities, for spouses to strike a deal on how to spend the money — one gambles, the other drinks. But too often there is not enough left for food for the children. Inevitably, the fighting starts when the money is gone. In the days when the place was run by the missionary, the Aborigines were required to perform totally unproductive tasks in the belief that this would this assist their conversion to Christianity. They are done with unproductive tasks these days, but there are not enough productive ones to take their place. When I asked one young boy what he wanted to do when he grew up, he pointed to the petrol station, one of the very few places offering the prospect of real work.

Peter Wallace, a born-again Christian with a liking for loud shirts, is acutely aware of the problems. He has been a drinker himself, and lost not only his son, but his father, his brother and an adopted brother to suicide. He had not shaved since his son's death in November and would not remove the beard for 12 months, when a smoking ceremony would be held to complete the grieving process. When I met him he had just won the local election, and was in the process of developing plans to create meaningful employment, reassert cultural values and a build a sense of confidence and empowerment in the community: plans broadly in line with Noel Pearson's partnership plan. He didn't have the luxury of time, he conceded, or much scope for error. 'The young people are watching. They're watching everything we do.'

Jay Burchill might just qualify was one of those 'young people'. A 34-year-old, he arrived while I was talking with Wallace and offered to accompany Alastair and me to Buru, or China Camp, about 250 kilometres north-west of Cairns. It is a place that one day might represent a model for other parts of the Cape and the country. Jay's grandfather, Billy Burchill, was one of three elders who led the fight to secure the lease to Buru in 1993. They were successful and the three were among the first to move back to their country. Jay went with them to help them out.

When we turned off the dirt road and commenced our ascent, the sign was straightforward enough: 'Beware. Dingo baits.' But there was no warning of the six, fast-flowing creeks that needed to be crossed to reach Buru, the home of Peter Fischer, an uncle of Noel Pearson. I'm not sure quite what I expected, but what I saw was compellingly attractive. Once you passed through the area of eerie white skeletons — where pastoralists poisoned the trees so the sunlight could touch the pastures — the country was lush and stunningly beautiful.

Peter, who is 82, lived alone in a shack he built himself of corrugated iron. His best mate, George Kulka, 84, lived in another house a kilometre away. None of the others lived within shouting distance of each other. This is in contrast with the high-density living at Wujal Wujal and other former missions, where the lack of distance between dwellings is an invitation to tension. The gardens here were well-tended, and Peter and George and the other families grew virtually all their own food.

'Here's something that we can make a job out of', Burchill said on the way up in the four-wheel drive. 'There's tourism in this place. There's cattle. There's timber works. Making traditional spears and stuff like that. That's what I want to see. Get my people off the streets. Having Bama [Aborigines] in the tourist industry, having them employed, that is one way of having reconciliation. Get tourists and take them through the bush, talking, breaking down barriers. That's what I'm looking at.'

It took a while to establish a rapport with Peter, but once he got going, his story was as simple as it was compelling. 'When we were little, we had a terrible spell up here with the police. Women and kids taken away. We was in the camps and one of my mates, his name was Ogilvey, same age as me, went out to see what the police was doing when they came. Well they grabbed him, took him to Yarrabah Mission. He cried his guts out and after two months he died. We was about five years old, a half-caste kid. Just like you take a young calf away from the mother. The old cow never went to school, but they're very intelligent with their calf. But we are human beings. What the white was doing to the black, they should be very ashamed about it.

Peter's life had been different. 'I didn't come out of the camp, and me and George here, we both grew up together. I never went to school, not one day. And that's why I turned out to be a good black man. I would have went to Palm Island or Yarrabah. I'd have been no good. I'd have been on the grog, gambling, doing a lot of silly things that the townies doing today. I grew up with the Germans, cattlemen and good farmers. They wouldn't let us go to any church or any missionary because they was going to spoil us — the same as they did to the other blacks. They kept us home all the time till we grow up to be a man. They were lovely persons. The government and the missionary and the police, they were the devil.

'Our people, the black, can be stupid person, give the police a hand [looking for us]. When the police came, we used to go down to the mouth of the Daintree River and live on mangoes. I grew up to be a hard-working man. I opened up the Daintree for fattenin' cattle, for the dairy and all that.'

'I know so many bad things that happened with the black people through the white. If I say the proper truth to you, what happened to the woman from the white man, you'd just get up and walk away. It's so bad. I can't bring that out today because I don't want to hurt no one's feelings.'

We talked about reconciliation, and the debate about history and the need to come to terms with it. He told me of a young prospector who had come and asked permission to camp on his land and become so entranced he stayed. The man now speaks Kuku Yalanji fluently and has become a kind of son to Fischer. 'He's a white man but he changed his life. He can see how black people's lives are. No bills to pay. Not in debt. He's not in trouble. That's the sort of life people are looking for today.'

One of the problems, according to Peter, was that with rare exceptions like his white friend, non-indigenous Australia had been reluctant to learn anything from the blackfella. 'Reconciliation? We don't understand this sort of thing. They keep changing it. We don't change it. We live with nature, our culture, that's all we live. European people destroying everything to buggery. They blaming us for cutting one tree to build a house and that. Europeans can be very mean and very greedy. We Kuku Yalanji people, one of the best black people you can find: kind, got a good heart with the people and try to look after the people, 'cos you must remember, we born to live and die. We can't take nothing with us.'

We talked through the afternoon and Peter walked me to his orchard, where I tasted five-sided fruit for the first time. Before I left, he expressed the hope that one day the black and white could sit down and 'work out how we can get things moving in a good way'. As he said farewell, the flooding creeks beckoning and the rain falling, he added: 'If you could only understand the Bama culture, you'd really fall for it'. Several months later I heard that George, who shared life's journey with Peter and described himself as simply 'a mate of the mountains', had passed away.

I finally checked into the Cairns Hilton on the Friday evening — and found a laundromat a short walk away. The next morning I visited the Yarrabah community, another former mission with a troubled history. I was there to meet Dave Patterson and Les Baird, who had been instrumental in reducing self-harm in that community. In 1995, when five people took their lives, Yarrabah had the highest suicide rate per capita in the world. When I visited, there had not been a suicide in the community since 1996, although Baird cautioned: 'We deal in crisis on a daily basis here'. In the months after my visit, there were two more suicides at Yarrabah.

Part of the life promotion program is a focus on being able to read the warning signs of someone who could be contemplating suicide, and then staying with that person until the danger passes. Part of it is convincing people that self-harm is not going to solve their problems. This has included setting up a men's group to talk about managing anger. Another part of it is providing interesting things for people to do, things taken for granted in mainstream society. It might be sport, art, hunting or something else. In 2000, Yarrabah was admitted to the Cairns District Rugby League competition, after 20 years of trying, and it is not unusual for half the community to turn out to watch the team train. As Patterson, a young man with a big, gappy smile, put it, 'When I look at it now compared with five or six years ago, community people these days are a lot more resilient'.

The Yarrabah approach has prompted many communities in Queensland and elsewhere to develop life promotion programs, and seek help from Patterson, Baird and Ernest Hunter, a psychiatrist who has worked closely with Aboriginal communities for many years.

I met Hunter, a lean, fit-looking man with a pony-tail, at his office in the University of Queensland's department of social and preventative medicine in Cairns the following day. He explained the link between the phenomenon of suicide in indigenous communities and the period of deregulation that began in the 1960s and accelerated with the passage of the 1967 referendum. Overwhelmingly, he said, suicide has involved young men of the first generation to grow up in a deregulated environment. They grew up in communities which had access to alcohol, but none of the discipline that was imposed by the missions, few of the job opportunities that had existed on stations, and no opportunity to pursue the dreams of the mainstream.

'Why young men?' he asked rhetorically. 'The thing most destabilised by deregulation was their role in controlling the sacred and the economic domains. The importance of the sacred domain has been massively undermined in terms of the decisions of everyday life, and control of the economic domain has been reversed. The major economic resource in indigenous Australia is now a woman with a child ... Because the welfare economy privileges women in ways it doesn't men.' The impact on the male identity on remote communities, he says, has been devastating.

On top of a loss of these roles is a loss of identity. 'The traditional processes that carried a young person into adulthood are gone, and they've been replaced with a variety of things including incarceration, normative rituals of violence, normative rituals of drinking. This is not unique to indigenous Australians.'

He described a study from over a decade ago, which identified people at risk of suicide in a particular community. Ten years later, a follow-up study found that more of those identified as at risk were dead than the others, but that they hadn't died by suicide. 'They died of violence, of liver failure, and that suggests these people are in a lifestyle of crisis, a lifestyle of risk', explained Hunter. 'To simply focus on suicide, rather than addressing the generalised risk is wrong. In the end it's about how you create an environment of nurture, and development of resilience and resourcefulness. It may involve crossing the bridge to reconciliation, but it's also about doing small things in the here and now, about looking at the horizon but taking one step at a time.'

Hunter is acutely aware of the situation in many areas, but remains convinced that the answers lie in communities being able to solve their problems. This is the view at the heart of Noel Pearson's partnership plan.

'It's important not to become fatalistic, or to see this as some endless downward spiral' says Hunter. 'Fatalism gets you nowhere and I can sit and tell you of lots of people who are doing much better. I think though there are areas of ghettoisation.'

Ironically, he believed some of the health professionals in indigenous communities are part of the problem. 'There's the old madmen, missionaries and misfits thing, but there's also a group who become quite angry and fatalistic and, for very personal reasons, stay and stay being angry and fatalistic — and infect people. Some of these people can't go anywhere else. Some become embittered gatekeepers and there are lots of embittered gatekeepers in indigenous Australia still. And there are gatekeepers in academia as well, academics who own a certain indigenous population or whatever. I think all of us in academia and in health services are part of that in some way or another.'

But he remains optimistic. 'There are lots of reasons to see things have changed. There is now a cadre of [indigenous] professionals largely in government service, but increasingly moving into private enterprise and other areas that just didn't exist before. And there's a bit of an irony here because through the 1980s and through the Royal Commission [into black deaths in custody] the statement was made to the Gary Foleys that if you really want to change things, go out there and get a degree and we'll talk about it.

And that happened. And then, around the time of Wik, suddenly we say, "Fuck the degree. We're going to legislate you out." There was a shift from protest to professionalism, and then the goalposts were moved. And what we've seen in the last three years is resurgent protest, very understandably. I see that protest as a good reason not to be fatalistic.'

Noel Pearson isn't fatalistic by any stretch of the imagination. Nor is he the only indigenous leader seeking a fundamental shift in the way governments and indigenous communities respond to the problems have accumulated over the decades and intensified since the 1967 referendum. But he has presented his case in the most forceful, the most fearless and the most provocative manner, both in describing the extent of the crisis and in articulating a solution.

Pearson's solution is based on the principle that the right to self-determination is ultimately the right to take responsibility. His central proposition is that if Aboriginal Australians are to survive as a people, they have to rid their communities of the passive welfare mentality that has taken hold since the period of deregulation. Without change, he argues that Cape York communities will become just like the Grassy Narrows Indian Community of Ontario, described so starkly in this passage from Anastasia Shkilnyk's 1985 book, *A Poison Stronger than Love*:

> I could never escape the feeling that I had been parachuted into a void — a drab and lifeless place in which the vital spark of life had gone out. It wasn't just the poverty of the place, the isolation, or even the lack of a decent bed that depressed me. I had seen worse material deprivation when I was working in squatter settlements around Santiago, Chile ... What struck me about Grassy Narrows was the numbness of the human spirit. There was an indifference, a listlessness, a total passivity that I could neither understand nor seem to do anything about. I had never seen such hopelessness anywhere in the Third World.

The passage is included in Pearson's recent publication *Our Right To Take Responsibility*, which also sets out his plan for developing a real economy for Aboriginal society, reviving the traditional subsistence economy, and turning all welfare programs to able-bodied Aboriginal people into 'reciprocity programs'.

I met Noel Pearson in the lobby of my hotel and walked to a nearby restaurant on a warm, windless night. He had just flown in from Brisbane and another round of discussions with Queensland Government officials. He was tired, frustrated and resolute. Same as he always was. We both ordered the seafood curry and a bottle of white wine, and left without emptying the bottle. I told him of my meeting with his uncle, and we discussed the paradox of the last 30 years: that the improvement in the material position of indigenous communities has led to a deterioration in their social position.

'I think back before welfare, government only saw the physical poverty, the material poverty of communities on the Cape. They never really understood that socially Aboriginal communities were rich. So they came in to fix this material poverty and started feeding people and building houses for them. Old Peter Fischer, my uncle up there, he built all those things himself. He feeds himself and that's how our communities were.'

Pearson himself grew up in a fibro hut in Hopevale, 'no electricity and a kerosene lamp, but it was the house my father built — and he repaired it. We ate bloody tripe and cattle bones for dinner most nights, but we didn't have diabetes, didn't suicide, didn't have petrol sniffing and things like that.'

'Now it's not that the material situation for Aboriginal society didn't need to be improved' he continues, 'It's just that the whole welfare state method was wrong, which was basically come in, change the place overnight. In fact [they told us] "You guys don't have to do much. We've got contract builders, bureaucracies who are going to feed you."' Pearson is very much against this approach. 'I know some of my convictions now sound terribly right-wing, terribly anti-government, but it's because the methods of the bureaucracy, especially in social policy, are just bloody terrible. If there's a problem you have to have a program and a bureaucrat. They're the two solutions. And nobody's thought about the fact that people need resources. How can we transfer resources other than through the program/bureaucrat model?'

Answering this question represents a fundamental challenge for governments and bureaucracies. Pearson was in no doubt that the key was to unlock the power in the money which governments are transferring to communities. 'At the moment the money is very destructive, and the clear evidence is that the day the family allowance comes to town is the day when the kids are most under threat from violence.'

The challenge, then, was to make the money an empowering resource, but one of the strongest lines of resistance was within the communities themselves. 'The ideological problem goes back to the [1967] referendum and the whole citizenship thing, because passive welfare was a gift of citizenship — that "No longer are you guys going to be discriminated against with unequal wages. We're going to make you citizens of Australia and we're going to give you passive welfare and, not only that, free access to the pub." The most insidious thing about welfare is that it's not like the external body blows of racism. The sticks and stones of racism are wounds that you suffer externally. The whole welfare thing is viral. It actually gets inside you and breaks you down from the inside, and that's what it's done in Aboriginal society. It's got into the culture. It's got into the relationships, the law, the ideology of the community — that to be a drunk is to be Aboriginal. And that's why passive welfare is so much harder to attack. To attack welfare is to attack the body in which that disease is situated.'

The main task, said Pearson, was to restore the values, social standards and expectations of Aboriginal society that have been eroded by welfare. 'We've got to have a return to the real Aboriginal culture. People who say to me it's Aboriginal to drink in the park in a mob are having me on, are trying to kid me about what real Aboriginal culture is, to manipulate me', he said. 'Real Aboriginal culture is not people sitting in a circle getting pissed while kids are going hungry. We've got to confront that manipulation. We've got to return to base one.' One of the ways to do this, was to empower those who are horrified at the collapse in values with the tools to restore them, especially the old people. This could mean communities deciding when and where alcohol can be consumed and having their decisions enforced by the white police in the community. But with responsibility, there needed to be incentive to change.

As Pearson expressed it, 'My father's generation, the people who became adults before 1970, they worked in a real economy for unequal wages or no wages. They were discriminated against and then the country said, "We'll get rid of discrimination, but sorry we can't find a place for you in the economy." In my view, reconciliation has got to be underwritten by a new economic deal. If we don't understand that "it's the economy, stupid", then it's just mere symbolism and fanfare and that's all reconciliation will ever be. It won't provide a real basis for inclusion.'

Pearson's vision is about children having 'orbits'. They could go away to study and to work, but not lose contact with their culture, their identity, their base. It was an area where new technology could play a crucial role, by giving people access to their stories, history and culture when they were a long way from home. It was an idea Pearson picked up from the Jews. 'They've kept their identity and community, but it's never stopped them from being at the cutting edge of what the Westerners were up to, you know, whether it's medical science, or literature or art. We've got to adopt a similar attitude.'

It is an idea that appeals to many young Aborigines, but is lived by all too few, largely because it is a challenge to traditional thinking. 'It's been hard with the elders, this orbit idea, because people want to keep their kids to themselves, hold them close', Pearson conceded. The strength of feeling was apparent last year when Pearson was selling the idea of orbits at the Wujal Land Summit. Peter Costello (the Cape York elder, not the federal treasurer) had a go at him, interjecting: 'You're wrong, mate. You don't look after your mother!'

Another attitudinal constraint is what Pearson called the 'big anti-intellectual thing' in the Aboriginal movement. 'It's really stunting the possibilities of what Aboriginal kids could achieve.' But the biggest frustration for Pearson over the last year had been the resistance from bureaucracy and those with a vested interest in things staying the same. 'The sheer vehemence of some of the campaigning that's gone on against the partnership plan has sat me back on my arse big time', he said. 'It only requires everybody to have a smidgen of negativity and you create an overwhelming weight against change.'

As for the Howard Government, Pearson said Australia would have to wait for another prime minister for a national understanding to be fully achieved. Perhaps surprisingly, this was not always his view. He told me he wrote John Howard a long letter after he came to power in 1996, arguing that the Keating Government had addressed the issue of rights and that Howard should move on to the issue of responsibility, without repudiating what had been achieved. By retreating on Mabo and winding back native title rights, Pearson said the Howard Government squandered the chance. 'It's a great pity, because it really needed a conservative government to embrace reconciliation, because that way you'd know you had 80 per cent of the country behind it.' The lack of national leadership, he argues, only increases the urgency to pursue a solid outcome in Cape York.

'I think the overriding truth is that the situation is bleak, but in that bleak situation you have got these great people, great sparks of hope. The problem is the good people on the ground, the great guys organising the CDEP, the great people doing something about the grog or petrol sniffing, are railing against the odds here. My main task is to create the space for them, the political and structural space for people to work out their own solutions.' The partnership plan was about turning those 'hopeful little sparks' into a raging, unstoppable fire, one that reverses the tide of welfare and alcohol dependency and provides a true basis for reconciliation.

Michael Gordon

Kenneth Jacob, chairman of the Mornington Island council and unassuming leader of his people, considers drugs, more than alcohol, are the problem leading to the suicides in his community.

4 Mornington Island to Doomadgee: The hangman's shadow

I'm going to see a lot of young people die before me, and it makes me sad. Kenneth Jacob, chairman, Mornington Shire Council

Reconciliation is never talked about here. We just kind of get on with day-to-day life and see things on the news. Helen Jones, Aboriginal Health, Doomadgee

When the debate about a treaty between indigenous and non-indigenous Australia was revived after the reconciliation walk across Sydney Harbour Bridge, the common response of opponents was that a treaty should be opposed because it implied an agreement between separate nations. I wonder how many of these critics have been to places like Mornington Island and Doomadgee. They are so removed from the Australia most of us take for granted that they could be provinces in an alien land.

My main preparation for visiting both communities was to read Rosalind Kidd's revealing investigation of the treatment of Aborigines in Queensland, *The Way We Civilise*, and to interview over the phone some of those who took part in a groundbreaking 1999 investigation of alcoholism and violence. This had been done by a task force of Aboriginal and Torres Strait Islander women, and chaired by Boni Robertson, a gently-spoken Aboriginal academic. The task force produced a report of around 400 pages and described the level of violence on communities as a national disgrace. 'The violence being witnessed can only be described as immeasurable and communities, pushed to the limit, are imploding under the strain', it said. There were dozens of recommendations, almost all of them expressed with a sense of urgency and aimed at giving the communities the tools to address their problems. All of them are consistent with the ideas in Noel Pearson's proposed partnership plan.

Some communities were identified in the report, others were not. One reference to Mornington Island was barely disguised. It said:

When a community has to deal with the tragic deaths of 24 young men in one year, most of which were suicides, there can be no stronger cry for help. Indeed, it is a deafening roar that something is desperately wrong. When the same community reports three men raping a three-month-old child, who was raped by another offender 10 days later, there is a crisis of huge proportions.

This same community has a $6 million tavern. The presence of the tavern ensures the continuation of devastating violence against vulnerable women and children. The modern hospital has the responsibility of stitching up physical wounds, setting broken bones and holding mutilated bodies in the morgue. Informants see the hospital as being like a fortress, protecting the workers from the virus of violence that infects the community. Even with the high rates of interpersonal violence, there are limited counselling services available in this community. It is a futile exercise to use public health resources for critical and much needed emergency care while ignoring the need for real health improvement through prevention initiatives.

The reference to Doomadgee, 150 kilometres south of the Gulf of Carpentaria, was also explicit. The community did not have a canteen selling alcohol, the report said, thanks only to the grace and tenacity of the lone woman on the council, Clara Foster, who had successfully blocked all endeavours by the other councillors and by state and federal bureaucrats to fund one:

In the early 'nineties, the Mt Isa ATSIC [Aboriginal and Torres Strait Islander Commission] regional office funded a consulting architect to travel to Doomadgee to begin the process of drawing up plans for a canteen. At around the same time, two children drowned in an open sewerage drain.

How do you compare the reality of these places with the picture that emerges from this report and many others? It's hard, not least because the violence and the misery is rarely in clear view. But it's even harder to comprehend what it must be like to grow up in a community where your best hope in life is not to be a doctor or a lawyer or a tradesman, but to get a job with the Aboriginal work-for-the-dole program, where prison is seen by many as one of life's initiations, and where all families are regularly touched by violent tragedy.

Is it as bleak as the portrait of the Grassy Narrows Indians of Ontario highlighted by Noel Pearson? No — not yet, at least. This is partly because you can see hope and resilience in the eyes of the young, even the 'lamppost children', those who are walking the streets at two in the morning because they fear going home.

Mornington Island, with a population of 1200, was a mission from 1914 until 1978. For much of this period, children were separated from their families and locked in dormitories overnight. Adults were required to make a long walk each day to attend the church on the top of a hill. Now the church is a library, without a librarian, and the daily walk for many is to the pub. Largely because of its remoteness, some estimates place Mornington Island 20 years behind other Aboriginal communities in Queensland. Doomadgee, with a population roughly the same, is in a similar situation.

At Mornington, I interviewed the council chairman, Kenneth Jacob, in the dilapidated house he shares with an extended family of about 20 people. I arrived at his front yard without warning and received a friendly greeting. He wore long pants, no shirt and a cowboy hat. His face looked older than his torso. We sat on an old rug outside his front door as light rain fell. He explained that he was there for his people. There is no front gate and anyone was welcome any time, even when they were drunk. At one point a naked toddler with a runny nose emerged from the dark inside with a cigarette. 'For mum?' he asked, before lighting it for the child to take to her mother.

A reformed drinker himself, Jacob didn't appear to think alcohol was as much a problem as drugs, which were 'buggering everything up'. The combination of the two, he said, helped explain the suicides. 'I'm going to see a lot of young people die before me, and it makes me sad', he said. 'They smoke and drink and don't care.'

What was the truth about Kenneth Jacob? According to several people I met on Mornington Island, he is an unpretentious leader who respects his people and reflects their will. Warren Wilkinson, a 29-year-old drug-and-alcohol worker who grew up on the island, was among those who was hopeful that Jacob would support new ideas to tackle alcohol abuse. I did not meet Wilkinson during my two days on Mornington. He was away at a conference on suicide in Melbourne. But his name kept cropping up when people spoke of how they were trying to change things, and I later had several conversations with him over the phone.

Three months after my visit, Wilkinson's faith was rewarded. The council approved a 90-day trial where the canteen opened at

1 pm instead of 10 am on Thursdays and Friday, the days the welfare cheques are paid. Light beer was a dollar cheaper than full strength beer. Figures are still being collated, but anecdotal evidence suggests the change has led to people going to work for at least part of these days, to improved school attendance, and to less violence and alcohol-related injury. One test for the council's resolve will be whether it reverts to the old ways when the trial ends. There has also been progress toward securing the funding to build an all-purpose recreation facility, a move pushed strongly by the recently formed life promotion team.

In Cairns, Ernest Hunter had told me how suicide tended to come in waves. The wave that engulfed Mornington Island was predicted by Annie Chong, the deputy chairperson of the community who was instrumental in setting up the women's shelter. She told the local police sergeant, John Herbert, late in 1999 that she could hear it approaching, like a storm. There were no signs she could point to, just a strong feeling. 'You wait. It will come like a sickness', she told him. In the four months before I arrived, four young men took their lives and there were at least as many attempted suicides. Was it over, I asked her. 'It's stopped for a little while now', she replied. The sickness had moved somewhere else.

'The hangman's in town.'

That's what they were saying. Someone saw him step off the plane from Mornington Island. A tall, black man nobody knew. The Doomadgee community debated his existence at two meetings the day before I arrived. Some were convinced he was real. Others said it was rubbish. No one disputed that Doomadgee had a problem.

In the previous seven days, nine young people had attempted suicide. Some of them were among those who attended the two meetings convened by the Aboriginal health team. Helen Jones, the team leader, took notes on the reasons for the sudden epidemic. They read like a kind of checklist of despair: down in the dumps, feel no hope, family argument, alcohol, division in community, finish school and hit brick wall, don't know who to turn to, peer pressure, copy cat.

But for Jones, the most disturbing aspect was that alcohol was *not* involved in several of the attempts. 'The people I spoke to in follow-up talked about having nothing to do, nowhere to go, no future', she said. 'That's the sort of thing they were saying. Nobody loves them. Nobody cares for them.'

I had left Mornington, a community grieving those who took their lives and those who died in a light plane crash late in 1999, and arrived in Doomadgee. I found a community in a state of almost perpetual crisis. Aside from the problem of the attempted suicides, relations between the community and the Queensland Health Department were extremely tense. The department had evacuated the staff from the Doomadgee Hospital some months earlier, a move that left the community without doctors and most nursing staff.

There was no room in the accommodation I thought I had organised through the CDEP, but the program's manager offered me a bed in his home. He and his wife had done voluntary work abroad after their children had grown up, but he had always wanted to assist Aboriginal communities. It was a demanding job, and in the two nights I spent with them, they were interrupted at all hours during the nights with requests to solve all manner of problems.

On the first morning I went to the council office, visited the school and finally knocked on the door of the temporary quarters of the Aboriginal health workers. A sign on the door urged residents to attend the meetings for the 'community suicide action plan' and carried the hint of desperation:

WE NEED ALL THE COMMUNITY'S SUPPORT.
EVERYBODY MUST HELP.
WE CAN NO LONGER DO IT ALONE.

Chris Toby, one of the younger members of the team, was polite but made no attempt to conceal his frustration that local solutions were undermined by the patronising attitude of outside authorities. 'The moment they see us trying to succeed by ourselves, they put barriers in our way to bring us down', he said.

That afternoon, I walked to where Auntie Hilyer Jonny lived near the outskirts of the community. Boni Robertson, who had chaired the task force investigating violence in communities, had told me of her courage and determination in turning her own home into a safe-house for women, but my attempts to contact her by phone all failed. When I knocked on her door, she was unprepared and did not wish to talk. We chatted outside for a while before she resumed cooking lunch for her large extended family.

Back at the Aboriginal health centre, Helen Jones suggested I pay a visit to Wadjularbinna, a Gungalidda elder who was visiting Doomadgee. A frail woman with a cast-iron will, she told me the message to white Australia from the suicides was that these people are profoundly unhappy. The response should be 'to get out here and talk about our law, our customs, our spiritual beliefs, the things that make us live'. Wadjularbinna was among the first of the children taken from their parents when the old Doomadgee mission was established by the Plymouth Brethren on the Gulf of Carpentaria in 1936. It moved 100 kilometres south after a bad cyclone. She has vivid memories of having her mouth washed out with soap for speaking her language, being treated as slave labor by the missionaries, and having her husband chosen for her.

Sitting on the balcony of a timber house, she told her own story. Her only joy, she said, came before the Japanese attacked in 1942, when an order was given for the smaller girls to be returned to their parents until the danger passed. 'It was only then that I realised I'd been taken from loving, caring parents and learned all these beautiful things about them and my culture.' She was still a teenager when she had to return to the dormitories of Doomadgee. She says she was forced into a marriage that saw her become a station manager's wife, with white domestic servants. 'I went from rags to riches and I lived a lie for 18 years. I walked away from it because I was empty inside.'

Wadjularbinna wrote a detailed report setting out the community's side of hospital evacuation of November 1999, accusing Queensland Health of an abuse of statutory duty of care equivalent to manslaughter. The report gave only one side, but it also underscored the problems created when essential services are administered by those who fly in and out, often without developing any real sense of trust with the community, and without the slightest sensitivity to indigenous culture. 'There is enough wisdom, experience and leadership in the community to revive the spiritual and cultural life of the community', she wrote, but it was the material services that were suffering.

Although the Doomadgee school had not had a forced transfer for three years, 40 to 50 per cent of the staff turns over each year, and many of the newcomers are young and inexperienced. At the hospital, where the graffiti in the outside toilet boasts 'big boys don't cry in Doomadgee', it is common for nurses to come in on six-week contracts, often without receiving any training in cultural awareness. Lack of understanding played a big role when tensions boiled over in November 1999.

According to Wadjularbinna's account, the episode followed a breakdown in negotiations about a new primary healthcare building and a longstanding lack of trust between the workers and the Aboriginal Health workers. Many Doomadgee people were nervous about going to the hospital because they could not develop trust with those who were there for brief periods. The community council had no say in the selection of hospital staff, and there was no genuine involvement by those employed by the hospital with the local community. 'Such involvement is actually discouraged', she wrote.

So what happened to trigger the episode? Wadjularbinna said it began on a Friday night when the Aboriginal health worker was told over the telephone by the Mt Isa district manager of some trouble at the hospital the previous evening. She went to the hospital to discuss the matter with the director of nursing, but there was a meeting in progress and she was told to go away. Her report maintained the only incident at the hospital that night was caused by a 13-year-old boy who had gone to the hospital bleeding from the face after receiving a thrashing from an uncle. The report continues:

> The boy was distressed and drunk and when he found the door locked and the sister inside could see him but would not come to open the door to attend to him, he hit the glass door with a hammer he was carrying. The boy was small and he could be easily controlled by an adult. In fact, he gave up the knife and hammer when asked. He had been trying to get attention to get help for his nose. There is no way that he was sufficient threat to justify flying the hospital staff out of Doomadgee the next day.

The episode prompted a lot of bad publicity for Doomadgee, described as 'Doom City' and 'the most depressing of all remote communities', but many now consider the evacuation was a massive over-reaction. It also highlighted the lack of support and training given to nurses for remote areas, and added weight to one of the main findings of a survey of nursing staff conducted by the Central Queensland University in 1998. That study concluded that:

> remote-area nurses are living with frequent threats to their personal safety whilst on duty, on call and off duty, and that violent incidents are often handled badly by employers, the community and the nurses themselves ... Apart from offers to evacuate, the respondents stated there was little or no support forthcoming from employers after incidents of violence were reported.

Craig Hilton, a rural GP by training with extensive experience in Western Australia, arrived at the hospital as its new medical superintendent in February and he conceded that there was a lot of healing to be done after the evacuation. He also confessed to being a little apprehensive before arriving at Doomadgee. 'Before I came here I was worried that I may be coming into a battle zone', he said, 'or coming into a community with a lot of hostility. But I've found to my surprise that people by and large were very welcoming, very accepting of anyone who wants to come in genuinely and is willing to listen and willing to help, anyone who is genuine enough to come in for the long haul, rather than in for a month and out again.'

The 'long haul' in Doomadgee is 12 months, and Hilton said he had made it one of his goals as medical superintendent, that 'an incident like that doesn't happen while I'm here'.

I flew out of Doomadgee, the community without a wet canteen, early on a Saturday morning and stopped over again at Mornington Island. One of the passengers was a teenage girl who was met at the airport by her extended family. I chatted with her grandmother while two toddlers sucked on a can of ginger beer. The girl produced a large bottle of Scotch from her bag, and proceeded to decant it into the softdrink bottles of those in the car. By the time they called me to reboard the plane, the bottle was half-empty.

Months later, I rang Helen Jones, to ask how negotiations with the hospital had progressed. My timing wasn't good. 'We've had seven deaths in the last four weeks', she said. 'Last week we had four funerals. I'm just looking at getting someone to help to do some debriefing of the [Aboriginal health] team to work through where we've been and where we're going. Everyone's a bit numb.'

'Suicides?', I asked.

'A couple. A couple of car accidents. A couple of natural causes. It was just everything.'

'Alcohol and violence play a part?'

'Yeah, probably. Usually do.'

On a more positive note, she told me that relations with the hospital appeared to be much improved. There was progress toward the construction of the new building for the Aboriginal health workers next to the hospital and, at Jones' initiative, an executive management team had been formed from senior people from the hospital and the Aboriginal health team to ensure better communications. There was even a realisation that the nurses who came in from outside could be educated by the health workers. A youth council had been set up with seven or eight kids as part of the suicide prevention strategy. Steps had been taken to clean the place up and facilitate some community discussion. Almost as an after-thought, she said there was another piece of good news: Doomadgee's 1100 residents could now buy fresh bread each day from the new bakery.

What was beyond question was that, in places like Mornington Island and Doomadgee, issues such as suicide and the quality of health services had more relevance and immediacy than reconcilia-tion. As Helen Jones put it, 'Reconciliation is never talked about here. We just kind of get on with day-to-day life and see things on the news.'

Scott Welsh

The death of a Yolngu teenager, whose funeral ceremonies stretched from Nhu-lumbuy back to her community of Gurrumurru, underscored the case for more interpreters to service the Territory's indige-nous communities.

5 Arnhem Land: Death in the Top End

To come up with a program such as an interpreter service, in the Northern Territory or elsewhere, to my mind is akin to providing a wheelchair for someone who should be able to walk. Denis Burke, NT Chief Minister

If there's not going to be a treaty, there's got to be something stronger than a treaty and backed by constitutional change to give sovereign rights so no mad politicians can change it when they think they don't like blackfellas. Galarrwuy Yunupingu, Nhulunbuy

From small things, big things grow. Banbapuy, Yirrkala

They gathered in the Nhulunbuy Hospital car-park early on a sunny afternoon, their faces painted white with ochre, to send a teenage girl on her final journey home. Under the custom of the Yolngu people, I cannot tell you her name, but I can tell you she died, too young, from a treatable disease, and suffered greatly because of her inadequate command of English, her second language.

In Aboriginal society, she was a daughter to two former Australians of the Year, Galarrwuy and Mandawuy Yunupingu (the balanda, or non-indigenous, would call her a niece). Both men assumed leadership roles during an age-old Arnhem Land ceremony that spanned three locations and several days. Outside the mortuary at the rear of the hospital, the men danced a dance of life, pulling imaginary anchors, ropes and chains that evoked the centuries-old trade between the Yolngu people and the Macassan seafarers from the south-eastern tip of Sulawesi (a sophisticated trade banned in 1907) and which is equated with the journey of the spirit through life, death and rebirth.

At the airport, the dancers used imaginary digging sticks to signify the return of the girl to her roots, before her body was gently transported from the back of a stationwagon to a light plane. The

61

women mourners didn't dance at either location. Their role, Mandawuy explained later, was to support and celebrate, and cry. 'When they cry, they heal', he said.

I didn't witness the ceremony that extended over the next few days at Gurrumurru, a homeland community some 300 kilometres south-west of Yirrkala, where the girl was laid to rest. But Mandawuy approached it with enthusiasm as well as sadness.

After weeks of being absorbed in a number of projects, including a new Yothu Yindi album, the process of grieving was also an opportunity to reconnect. 'I'm going back to re-educate myself, to spiritually empower myself', he said.

It wasn't until later that I managed to contact Dr Paul Snelling, who treated the girl in intensive care after her arrival at Royal Darwin Hospital in February. She had been gravely ill with systemic lupus erythemetous, an auto-immune disease. He confirmed the truth of what others had told me, that better communication may well have prolonged her life and reduced her suffering. 'It was certainly a major factor in why she presented late and extremely unwell — because no one really understood how sick she was to begin with and how often and how aggressively she needed to be cared for', he said. 'She wouldn't be cured. Most of the diseases we deal with here you never cure, but you do manage and damp down. With her disease, if it was well treated and there were no problems, she would have a lifespan of at least [another] 20 or 30 years, one would have hoped. She was only 18.'

Dr Snelling said the girl's case was a good example of why he and others had sought, and received, approval for a study to demonstrate the impact interpreters would have on health outcomes in the Northern Territory. 'Even though the patient and the family spoke what was thought to be relatively good English, understanding isn't necessarily the same', he said.

The lack of indigenous interpreter services in the Northern Territory health system was raised in the Territory's Assembly late in 1999, when Chief Minister Denis Burke was asked about a woman who underwent a caesarian section without the proper consent being obtained. Burke's response was an indication of the elusive nature of reconciliation in remote Australia. Declaring it was time for some plain-speaking, he said it was a disgrace that Aboriginal people who had been exposed to ten years of schooling should require interpreters. 'To come up with a program such as an interpreter service, in the Northern Territory or elsewhere, to my mind is akin to providing a wheelchair for someone who should be able to walk', he said.

A year later, and more than six months after I attended the first stages of the young girl's funeral, two interpreters were due to start work at the Royal Darwin Hospital. A modest sign of progress.

Oscar Whitehead was the first person to tell me the girl's story. He was sitting with Andrea Collins and Gatjil Djerrkura in the restaurant at the Nhulunbuy Resort Hotel the night I arrived. I knew and respected Gatjil from his days as chairman of ATSIC. Andrea didn't know me at all, but generously became my guide over the next few days. Gapirri, her ten-year-old son, tagged along. I didn't see Oscar again until I arrived at Darwin, where he was completing his clinical placement as a third-year medical student at the hospital. It was then that he told me his own story.

Almost ten years ago, he was a young middle-class man in Melbourne, studying arts at Melbourne University and demonstrating a flair for linguistics. Then he met Raymattja, a woman from Arnhem Land who had come to Melbourne as part of her own work toward a graduate diploma of education and training. She ran a five-week course in Rirratjingu, her language, and Aboriginal culture. Oscar was among those who took her class. It was his first contact with Aboriginal people and, apart from finding her an inspirational teacher, he struck up a friendship with her husband, Nanikiya, a ranger who offered toward the end of their stay to adopt him as a brother. 'All my brothers are tall and thin', he told Oscar, who matched the description perfectly.

During the end-of-year break from university, Oscar decided to visit his new family and landed in Darwin with three telephone numbers, only to discover one had been cut-off, one was constantly engaged and the other simply rang out. It was two weeks before the third number was finally answered by Raymattja's sister, Banbapuy. Arrangements were made and Oscar flew to Nhulunbuy to be greeted by Nanikiya. Nanikiya took him to the Yirrkala community at dusk to be introduced, as his brother, to 30 or 40 people. There were so many unfamiliar names that Oscar tried instead to remember relationships, which were clearly more important. 'See that woman over there, the one with the blue top', someone said, 'She's your mother-in-law. You can't look at her.'

That's how it began. The biggest of many culture shocks came when he went hunting for stingrays with spears made especially for the occasion that afternoon, and returned to be tutored in a preparation that is very traditional. The liver, bile and gall bladder are removed before the stingray is boiled, and the cooked flesh stripped

63

away from the cartilage and mixed into balls with the uncooked liver. There were strict protocols on who was to be served first and when. But the surprise for Oscar was to see the young children walking around with their stingray balls in one hand and a can of Coke in the other, two icons of two very different cultures.

The other thing that happened on that first two-month visit was that Oscar and Banbapuy began to fall in love.

Then he returned to Melbourne to prepare for what he hoped would become a masters degree in linguistics: six or seven months of field work, documenting the language of the Garig people at Coburg, a big peninsula near the north-western corner of Arnhem Land, pointing north-west to the Tiwi Islands. His aim was to study cognitive science, where linguists work together with psychologists and others to develop theories on how humans process information, and then to complete his PhD at Edinburgh. But, from the moment Oscar arrived, he began to have doubts about the morality of the undertaking. When he was introduced to Nelson, the elder he would spend most his days with at Coburg, it was clear that the old man had only been given a fleeting idea of what the project was, how long it would take and what would become of the information Oscar took back to Melbourne. Yet he welcomed him without hesitation.

Oscar's supervisor had called it 'field work', and the word had implanted the image in Oscar's brain of arriving at a meadow, neatly fenced, to undertake his research, if not aloof, certainly detached from the lives of those who spoke the language he was to document. But it wasn't a field. It was a community of people with their own ideas and ambitions and agendas, a community where it was impossible to live without being drawn into the richness of the culture and the rituals that were part of survival. So he mixed linguistics with learning how to fix the generator and the solar bore, how to identify the plants that made up the rainforest, how to prepare a magpie goose for eating without using a knife; how to pluck it, which joints to break, how to open it so it was flat and could be cooked evenly.

The Garig language is very complicated and in the early weeks Oscar would sit for hours with the ever-patient Nelson, taping the numerous versions of each verb, which depend on the pronoun, until finally Nelson said: 'This no good. You're not learning properly.' He then took charge, at least in the mornings, teaching conversational phrases over a big tin of tea in an open-sided kitchen looking out toward Seven Spirit Bay.

'How are you?'

'Very good.'

'There's a boat.'

'Hmmm. There's another one.'

'This tea is good, eh?'

'Three boats now.'

And so it went. When anyone came to visit the community, they would inevitably ask Nelson who was this whitefella.

'He's no whitefella', would come the reply. 'He's a proper black-fella and Garig man and he talk with Garig language.' Nelson would then call Oscar over and demonstrate, usually by asking how many boats there were on the horizon, before dismissing him. Although these episodes had a comic dimension, Oscar could see that they gave Nelson a satisfaction, enhancing his self-esteem and perhaps his status in the community as well. Ultimately, they strengthened Oscar's views about the importance of language in Aboriginal culture, how it identified people and represented knowledge, how it was something to be valued, and guarded.

Over dinner in Darwin, Oscar explained his predicament in these terms. 'I'd been sent up there to get all this knowledge about a language hardly anyone knew about, and as soon as you write anything down as a thesis it becomes the property of the university. I didn't think that was a good deal. Then there was the fact that the people in the community didn't really know what was going on. I was going to go up there, take away all this stuff and nobody knows what will become of it, and I get a nice piece of paper out of it, a stepping-stone to somewhere else.'

When he returned to Melbourne with his tapes and notes he deferred his course, later accepting Banbapuy's invitation to join her at Yirrkala. They married in 1997 and Oscar began studying medicine the following year. One of his aims is to reduce the risk of the kind of communication breakdown that prematurely ended the life of the young girl.

Andrea Collins, one of four former wives of Galarrwuy, became my point of contact with the Yunupingus, although it seemed clear from the start that the girl's funeral made this a difficult time to spend time with them. Andrea was born at the Cherbourg Aboriginal Settlement in Queensland, and her father played rugby with Frank 'Big Shot' Fisher, the legendary grandfather of Cathy Freeman. The morning after I arrived, she showed me the sites with Gapirri: the sprawling conveyor belt from the Nabalco mine to the port, the Yirrkala and Marngarr communities, the spot under the tamarind tree where the Yolgnu people told the Macassars not to return after their trade in trepang (or beche-de-mer), pearls, turtle shells and other goods was terminated by the Australian Government. I also saw Galuru, the beach where Gapirri liked to go swimming and walking with Frank Brennan, the Jesuit social justice campaigner, whenever he came up.

Gapirri, Galarrwuy's fifth son, was preparing for his initiation, having been taught by his father to spear stingray, catch turtles and hunt kangaroo and emu. He had also been out bush and shown how to treat cuts, and been assigned the important task of protecting the body during a funeral. He felt he was ready.

We were driving back to Nhulunbuy when Manduwuy appeared from the opposite direction and told Andrea the ceremony for the dead girl would be held later that afternoon. What was not immediately clear was that Andrea's stationwagon would be required to transport the body from the hospital to the airstrip. At the hospital, 30 or 40 people had already gathered and they moved around the back when Manduwuy and Galarrwuy appeared, Manduwuy in an old 'Rip Curl' T-shirt, boardshorts and bare feet. When the designated vehicle failed to arrive, Andrea drove the stationwagon to the airstrip and Gapirri and I travelled with Galarrwuy, who seemed in a trance, oblivious to my presence.

I saw the brothers the next day, before they left for Gurrumurru. We met at the yacht club established by Nabalco to service its workforce. The company, said Galarrwuy, had been squatting on the land for the past ten years. Now they were talking about making a proper settlement. The club was likely to be renamed Manyimi Yacht Club, traditional owners would have a role on the committee and a plaque would be placed honoring the Yunupingus' father, Munggurawuy, for his role in the struggle for land rights.

With other Yolgnu leaders, Munggurawuy led the unsuccessful fight against Nabalco while the company was negotiating with the Federal Government to excise a large bauxite-rich portion of Aboriginal land on the Gove Peninsula. Throughout negotiations lasting from 1965 until 1968, the company never communicated with the Yolngu people. Munggurawuy was also one of the plaintiffs in the unsuccessful court action that followed. His son, Galarrwuy, was one of the interpreters in the court. Although Justice Blackburn upheld the idea that the land was empty at the time of British annexation, there was much in the judgment that paved the way for the lie of 'terra nullius' to be subsequently laid to rest.

In particular, he found that the Yirrkala Aborigines formed a community which was in principle definable; that they had a system of law which they accepted as obligatory upon them; that the system of law was cognisable as such in the courts; that the Aborigines thought of land in the Gove Peninsula as consisting of tracts each linked to a clan; that each clan regarded itself as a spiritual entity with a practical relationship to particular areas; and that each clan had a religious duty to care for and to tend its land — a duty the mine prevented from being carried out.

When he delivered the 1998 Vincent Lingiari Memorial Lecture, Galarrwuy traced the start of their struggle against the bauxite mine to the damage done by the mining company to the sacred banyan tree at Nhulunbuy. He had been taken to the tree by his father, and said it was the first time he saw him with tears in his eyes.

'I was shocked. I had never seen my father in the position of not being able to stop someone doing something in our country. His authority had been absolute and now this mining company and these balanda were ignoring us. The tree is a special place — inside it are important things. It's like the heart of the country. Our beliefs about our land reside in that tree and at the site of the tree. They reside in the rocks, in the water and in our minds. We know these things to be true … We often spoke about the Yolgnu people as that tree: strong and firm and fixed to the land. He told me Yolgnu people were stuck deep into the land. He told me I should never forget this moment because it would test all of the skill and the knowledge of the Yolgnu people. It was only at that moment we understood that in the eyes of the balanda law we were no-one. Our ancient laws and our social systems were invisible to the legal and political system which had total power over our lives.'

More than two weeks later in Broome, I met Pat Dodson. He recalled a meeting between indigenous leaders and the mining company executives. They were all seated in a circle and, to break the ice, each person gave a summary of who they were and where they were coming from. 'The first one introduced himself, saying "I'm Billy Bloggs. I've got $X million under investment, X tonnage coming out of this mine, $X million earmarked for exploration in the next two quarters. That's me." When it came to Galarrwuy, he says, "I come from Gove, and my billabong, which my father showed me as a kid, has been destroyed and that's a big worry to me because I can't teach my kids about the important places". Two very different perspectives of life. It was only when one of the other mining guys said to Galarrwuy, "We're two grandfathers", that it started to become human, that there was a basis for discussion.'

Galarrwuy was a member of the Council for Aboriginal Reconciliation for three years, but resigned soon after the Howard Government came to power in 1996 in protest at budget cuts to ATSIC. He believes subsequent events have vindicated his decision. 'Everything since then has just bitten people's bums', he said.

Convinced that the ten-year process for reconciliation had failed, Galarrwuy believed the Corroboree 2000 that would be held in Sydney in a few weeks (May 27-28) should mark the beginning of a new push for a formal agreement between indigenous Australia and the balanda. 'Practical reconciliation is as simple as saying sorry', he said. 'If you start doing that, maybe you can soften some of the hard core politics. It's nothing to do with hard core political. This has got to do with humanity.' These words were directed at John Howard. Yunupingu's message was that symbolic and emotional gestures can indeed be practical. It was hardly a new idea, and I found it expressed with eloquence and power in the latest collection of writing by Raymond Carver, *Call Me If You Need Me.* In one passage, Carver meditates on this line of prose from the writings of Saint Teresa, who lived 373 years earlier: 'Words lead to deeds … they prepare the soul, make it ready, and move it to tenderness'. Words lead to deeds.

Galarrwuy said he had hoped the ten-year formal process of reconciliation would produce something concrete. Now it was time for a new process that would deliver. 'One important thing I would like to say is this: I'm not encouraging our people to wave flags anymore. Those years are over. We have established who we are. Canberra knows who we are. They're just frightened to come to the party. It takes real courage from John Howard or any other prime minister to come to our camp and say, "Let's fix this once and for all". If there's not going to be a treaty, there's got to be something stronger than a treaty and backed by constitutional change to give sovereign rights so no mad politicians can change it when they think they don't like blackfellas. The nineteenth century never worked for blackfellas. The twentieth century didn't. The new century should.'

Just over two years earlier, in his only visit to an Aboriginal community, John Howard came to Yirrkala as a guest of Galarrwuy and Djerrkura. He witnessed a ceremony no other white man had been privileged to see, and spent time at Djerrkura's home at Yirrkala, overlooking the Arafura Sea. While Howard later described the visit as a highlight of his prime ministership, his hosts remain convinced that the prime minister failed to reciprocate the generosity and respect afforded to him. 'I knew that we were entertaining somebody who never understood, or pretended not to understand', said Galarrwuy.

That night, I was a guest a Djerrkura's home at Yirrkala, and was able to take in the view that so impressed the prime minister. In the late afternoon, we walked to the spot where the ashes of Nugget Coombes were spread, and Djerrkura spoke of plans to have a fitting memorial erected. Later, sitting on the veranda at his home, Djerrkura argued that Howard's failure to 'show leadership based on conscience' had placed a limit on what could be achieved.

'What we're seeing is the old mentality, where the white man knows what's best for Aboriginal people, rather than the white man asking Aboriginal people what is best for them', he said.

Before leaving the Gove Peninsula, I met a group of Yolngu women under the trees at Shady Beach. Most of them were teachers and they seemed more optimistic than their tribal elders, perhaps because they had recently experienced a reconciliation event at the Nhulunbuy School, and been impressed by the hunger for knowledge of the balanda children about indigenous culture and history. It demonstrated the progress since the year before, when a white Nhulunbuy resident admitted he had lived in the town for 14 years and not once visited the Yirrkala community.

Among them was Raymattja, who made such a profound impression on Oscar Whitehead almost ten years earlier. Her own father, Roy Marika, had instigated the historic court action against Nabalco, and Munggurawuy, Galarrwuy's father, was her maternal grandfather. She remarked with understated pride that several of the students who took that five-week course were now working for Aboriginal causes and organisations. 'I think I converted them', she said. One of the positive changes since then has been the increase in the number of indigenous teachers at universities, teachers like Marcia Langton at the University of Melbourne. 'We see a lot of balanda people changing their views and getting on well with Aboriginal people. That's reconciliation.'

I asked why the culture seemed so much stronger here than other places. 'The people have preserved and maintained their language and their culture', Raymattja said, conceding that the influence of the church had not been as destructive here and that the area was less affected by the practice of removing children from their parents. Banbapuy, who was introduced to Oscar at Shady Beach, encapsulated the mood of optimism of the women, adapting the words of the Paul Kelly song: 'From small things, big things grow'.

Michael Gordon

Jack Long, taken from his central desert home and raised on the Tiwi Islands, is typical example of the stolen generation.

6 Tiwi Islands: In the tracks of tears

Mr Howard, if you just walked in their shoes you would understand. Michael Long, Melbourne

If the Government is really committed to reducing Aboriginal morbidity, they will need to think in terms of a much higher level of funding. Bill Barclay, Tiwi Health Board

The Government thought they were creating a welfare net under people. In fact, they were creating hammocks. Bob Beadman, NT Department of Local Government

Jack Long stood with his shovel, barely 20 metres from the spot where the lugger came in 60 years ago to deliver him — a two-year-old child whisked away from his parents, never to see them again — to the Tiwi Islands. He's a proud man, Jack. You can see it in his eyes. But you can see other things, too. Like pain, suffering, strength, resilience and forgiveness. Maybe even anger, too. Unresolved anger. Just now, it's pride. He is most proud of his son, Michael, one of the Essendon Football Club's on-field leaders. Kathy Rioli, another of Jack's children, and just as proud of Michael, took me to meet him on Melville Island during one of the most remarkable single days of my journey.

I came to Melville, the second-largest island in Australia, to witness the decision by the four Tiwi communities to form a new system of regional government as part of a wider agenda to tackle their problems. In March, I had written to the chairman of the Tiwi Land Council, Matthew Wonaeamirri, as I had to the other communities, seeking permission to visit. He had responded with an invitation to observe history being made. He also went to some effort to explain how the Tiwis were trying to build more economic independence through joint ventures in tree farming and aquaculture.

'We are beset by many of the same problems of other Aboriginal people', he wrote in his letter. 'Our advantages seem to be that we have always considered we owned our land. We are a one-language, homogeneous group. We have been able, to some extent, to retain our pride and identity as island people.' Many of their problems stemmed from the fact that five generations had accepted that authority belonged to the state 'and that our leaders are accountable to the state, rather than their own people, for the development of Tiwi society'.

Kathy prepared and served the lunch and then gave me a tour of the local community, Pirlangimpi, where her husband Cyril Rioli Jnr, was the council president. The Riolis and the Longs are two of the more famous names on the Tiwis — and in AFL football. Maurice Rioli was one of the indigenous trail blazers, and now Dean Rioli had joined Michael Long at Essendon. Outside the council building, a younger Rioli was playing kick-to-kick with a friend. At the beach, I saw Sebastian Rioli, father of Dean, setting a fishing net with a group of children.

Less than a fortnight before my arrival here, the Howard Government had responded to a Senate inquiry into the stolen generation with a detailed submission asserting there was in fact no such thing. In the executive summary, the government's submission said:

> The proportion of separated children was no more than 10 per cent, including those who were not forcibly separated and those who were forcibly separated for good reason, as occurs under child welfare policies today. There was never a 'generation' of stolen children. The category of persons commonly characterised as separated (or 'stolen') combines and confuses those separated from their families with and without consent, and with and without good reason.

The language was so icy cold and so utterly insensitive that it gave the impression it was calculated either to rub salt into the wounds of the stolen or to strike a chord with those without sympathy — the Pauline Hanson mob. Either way, it was always going to generate controversy and set back the cause of reconciliation.

While insisting it was not seeking to defend or justify past practices, the submission went on to assert that 'the nature and intent of those events have been misrepresented, and that the treatment of separated children was essentially lawful and benign in intent and also reflected wider values applying to that era'.

Michael Long responded a few days later by writing an open letter to John Howard in *The Age*. It helps to explain his father's pride:

Dear Mr Howard,

How do I tell my mother that Mr Howard said the stolen generation never took place? How does he explain to me why none of my grandparents are alive?

How do I explain to my mother, who as the most loved, trusting mother figure to all who knew her that Mr Howard is just the same as the people who were in power then, cold-hearted pricks.

How do I tell my mother that her grandchildren were never affected by the stolen generation, that they don't know their aunties and uncles, their people?

Does Mr Howard understand how much trauma my grandmother suffered. It ripped her heart out, what she went through. Even when she died, her baby was never returned home.

If you put yourself in their shoes — I have three children — and people come knocking at my door, grabbing my children, putting them in the back of a truck, yelling, screaming. Over my dead body, Mr Howard.

Back then my mother had no choice but to go. It was wrong. It did happen. It was Government policy.

My mother was taken when she was a baby, taken to Darwin and put in a boat — she had never seen the sea before — screaming and yelling, not knowing what was happening and then crying herself to sleep. I call that trauma and abuse. I am so angry anyone could do this to a child just because their skin was a different colour.

Mr Howard, I can't tell my mother because she has been dead for 17 years. Who is going to tell her story, the trauma and lies associated with her people and their families? Mr Howard, if you just walked in their shoes you would understand.

I am all for reconciliation, Mr Howard. I am part of the stolen generation. It's like dropping a rock in a pool of water and it has a rippling effect, so don't tell me it affects 10 per cent. No amount of money can replace what your Government has done to my family.

Two days after the letter was published, and read into the record of Federal Parliament, Howard apologised to those who had been offended by the submission.

Now, a stone's throw from where his own boat came in, Jack told me his own story, how he had a white father (half English, half Chinese) and a full-blood Aboriginal mother, and how for years he had hated his dad for not coming to get him. It was only 18 months ago, after he gained access to the archive material, that Jack discovered the truth. His father had fought unsuccessfully for custody of his son, and his letters had been burned by the nuns. 'Now I forgive him, but I never even saw him', Jack said, his eyes moist with the memory.

Jack Long is a brave man who has played 300 games of senior football for St Mary's in Darwin. But he was too apprehensive, even after learning the truth, to return to Ti-Tree, 250 kilometres north of

Alice Springs, where he was born and stolen because he was a half-caste. Jack was all for reconciliation, too. He said heaps of his friends were white, and he considered his son a true leader and role model. 'Michael's doing it not just for himself, but for every Aboriginal person and white person, so we can all communicate', he said.

Kathy introduced me to others who had been taken, like Peter Brogan, a community elder. He told how he had gone to his birth place to find his mother, only to discover she had died. His full-blood brothers and sisters referred him to an old man with failing eye-sight, who asked him to remove his shirt. 'He had a good look at my back and said, "Yeah. You're the one. I know you."' The old man then told him how his mother had used charcoal to blacken his face before the authorities came, and how they used a rag to clean it and discover his lighter skin. 'My mother was screaming, trying to pull me back. They just took off.'

Peter Brogan has never had a drink in his life and says he has no idea what would have become of him if he had stayed. 'I can forgive', he told me. 'I'm not that bad.'

Back at the council, the meeting was discussing progress with plans to develop plantation forestry and a barramundi farm to provide much-needed employment on Melville and Bathurst Islands. Under the agenda item on aquaculture was the annotation: 'Emelio the prawn farmer is still coming'.

They're a proactive mob, the Tiwis, and their leaders appeared to be tackling their problems with the sort of single-minded ferocity Long displayed on the football field. Consider three examples.

Back in 1997, the Tiwis were included in four co-ordinated health care trials in indigenous communities. Medical and pharmaceutical benefits were pooled and cashed out to give local authorities flexibility in tackling chronic problems like heart and kidney disease and diabetes. They established a 'Tiwi for life' public health program, increased the number of indigenous nurses, and doubled the number of days the islands had access to doctors. They also embarked on an aggressive assault on escalating levels of renal failure, heart disease and diabetes. As a result, there was a dramatic drop in the incidence of scabies, one of the first points of entry for renal disease. The trial is one of the reasons why deaths from all causes in the Tiwis had fallen by a third in the past four years.

When the trial was coming to an end late in 1999, federal health officials based in Darwin warned the community that the program would be reviewed and there was no guarantee about the future. As the health minister, Dr Michael Wooldridge, told the story, 'They were literally on the next plane to Canberra and camping in my ante room until I'd see them. They were so positive about it, so willing to fight for it, that I've been prepared to back them and find the money to keep it going.' Wooldridge had since backed a $330 000 program to prevent suicide that was seen as an unqualified success, but the funding would run out at the end of the year, and, once again, the locals were anxious about whether they would be able to keep the program going.

The second example concerns the response of Northern Territory police to a coroner's call in November 1999 for a police presence in Nguiu on Bathurst Island, where youth suicide had been a major problem. When the commissioner proposed simply increasing the number of visits by police based on Melville Island, the Tiwi leaders said it was totally unacceptable. Within a week, he came back with a promise of a police presence from Tuesdays to Saturdays. Since then, work on the construction of two houses has begun at Nguiu and there are plans to have two police on the island full-time.

The third example is the decision to embrace a new system of regional governance, offering economies of scale and the prospect of more autonomy. The concept was to establish a framework that incorporated traditional decision-making based on land tenure, but was able to use economies of scale to assume increasing responsibility from ATSIC and the Commonwealth. The ultimate aim is to break the cycle of welfare dependence. Like any rationalisation, it involves a willingness of local leaders to surrender a degree of their autonomy for the greater good. Bob Beadman, the head of the NT Department of Local Government, told the meeting they had taken 'a momentous step', and promised his support. At the meeting, Beadman felt the need more than once to reassure the leaders that there were no hidden motives on the part of the Territory Government. 'What we're after is a better result for indigenous communities', he said.

While it would be nice for the Tiwis to be the first indigenous group to move to regional government, Beadman told them they were not alone. They were in front of the pack that included the Jawoyn mob, the people in East Arnhem, and those north-west of Alice Springs. But being first would give them added credibility, and mean even more weight would be given to community ideas, he said. The hard work had been done.

Although each of the examples demonstrates a capacity to achieve, the Tiwis were frustrated that even where solutions were clear, the necessary resources were often not available. The initial response to the coroner's report, for instance, was to fly a policeman into Bathurst from Tuesdays to Saturdays, an unsatisfactory and stop-gap arrangement for him and the community.

And while Wooldridge has strongly supported their efforts to improve health, the Tiwis argue that their level of funding should be greater than the average because of the magnitude of their problems. It's an argument that has application to many remote indigenous communities. As Bill Barclay, the chief executive of the Tiwi Health Board Trust put it: 'Out of desperation we came up with this awful expression, the morbidity multiplier. What we're saying is that if the Government is really committed to reducing Aboriginal morbidity, they will need to think in terms of a much higher level of funding.'

It is an approach supported by a report undertaken for the Australian Medical Association by the respected health economist, Professor John Deeble. He outlined a 'very defensible case' for a needs-based increase of $240 million a year in the Aboriginal health budget. Spending would increase from an extra 8 cents for every dollar spent on non-indigenous health to an extra 36 cents.

Wooldridge was sympathetic, but responded:

Yes, there is a morbidity multiplier and yes, if you were funding on the basis of sickness, which we don't do anywhere else in the country, you'd put a lot more money in. But you also look at the mistakes of the past and money alone is not going to solve this. [Sir] Gus Nossal recently said we need to spend an extra hundred million over the next five years. The forward estimates provide for an extra $105 million. So the money is growing rapidly, but not instantaneously, because we want to put it into areas where the preparatory work has been done and the extra money is going to make a difference.

Aside from chronic disease, the Tiwi health problems include tooth decay among children, exacerbated because there is no fluoride in the water supply, and the high incidence of 'otitus media', an ear infection that causes profound hearing loss. In a Grade-Four class last year, clinicians found 90 per cent of the children had no eardrums. 2000 was designated the year of the ear, and Barclay said the health board was hoping for a major breakthrough.

Then there was the problem of youth suicide, reflecting a social malaise that asserted itself in alcohol and drug abuse and domestic violence. Since the coroner's inquest into four deaths in 1998, there

had been two more suicides, one of them an Aboriginal health worker. Part of the explanation to emerge from the investigation by
Coroner Greg Cavanagh was that these young Australians were
acutely aware of what the country had to offer, but felt excluded
from participation by forces totally beyond their control. His report
told how he was impressed by the intelligence, sense of humour,
enthusiasm and potential of the youth of the island, as well as their
ambition and career aspirations. He wrote:

> They watch the same television programs that a lot of urban city dwellers watch and
> I am sure have a lot of the same dreams as any other group of young people around
> Australia. What is their future in terms of career aspirations and dreams on the
> islands? I very much suspect that for the same reasons that suicide rates among
> young people are higher in rural areas of Australia, so is the case in the Tiwi Islands.
> That is to say, in my view, problems such as unfulfilled potential, frustrated ambi-
> tion, boredom, unemployment and non-achievement in terms of career aspirations
> all play a part in suicide and self-harm statistics. This problem is more evident on
> the Tiwi Islands than some other less functional Aboriginal communities in similarly
> remote locations precisely because many Tiwi Islanders are relatively better edu-
> cated and exposed to Western ideals which are not currently available on the
> islands.

Whether the problem of frustrated ambition is greater in communities with more exposure to Western ideals is a worthy subject
for research, but I have no doubt that Cavanagh's central point is
right. It was put to me in other ways by indigenous and non-indigenous people in other places, most concisely by Harry Scott at
Titjikala: 'Young suicides aren't coming from the no-hopers', he said.
'It's from those who feel and think.'

The Tiwis were working hard to address the problem of self-
harm, and had resorted to some extreme measures, like installing
wire 'crowns of thorns' on the power poles on Bathurst Island to stop
the children climbing them and threatening to commit suicide. Two
conversations I had after the meeting had broken up confirmed the
magnitude of the task. The first was with Barry Puruntatameri, the
council president of the Nguiu community, a big man with very dark
skin, thick black hair and a shy smile. We had not met during the
day, and I went up to him afterwards at the airport, as he waited for
his light plane to take him the short distance to Bathurst and I waited for mine to return to Darwin.

'The suicide problem is very bad', he said when I raised the subject. 'Last night there was three of them tried to harm themselves,

went bush. One boy climb up the big tree and we found him. A person got up really quick and cut the rope. He was flown to Darwin today. The other two was all right. They were doing the same. This is going to be an ongoing thing. That's why we're tackling it.'

I asked why they were resorting to suicide.

'Nothing to look forward to. They go and ask mum for $20 to buy gunga and she refuse and the young people say, "I'll go hang myself". Some have done it already. There's just no education at home, nothing from the parents. These young people, they need love from parents.'

Before they started putting the wire around the power poles, Barry said the power used to be turned off regularly. 'You wouldn't believe this', he said. 'I've witnessed every one of them. They just swing like little flying foxes, you know, swinging from line to line. One fella [recently] escaped, nearly died. It's unreal.'

Barry then pointed me in the direction of Stanley Tipungwuti, the council president for the Wurankuwu community on Bathurst. He is a black man with a whitening beard, and wore a 'vote yes for our republic' T-shirt. He told me of an incident in his community the previous night. 'This boy climbed the power line. He wanted to buy gunga from a bloke who said, "No, you'll have to give me cash". And he said, "If you won't give me, I'll climb up and kill myself." My wife — she hasn't had a drink for three months — she got up and told him, "Don't do that! You're too young to die." He believed her and he got down.'

There was a surreal dimension to both discussions. We had spent the day discussing the plans for regional government and the progress toward the barramundi farm, and now both men were preparing to return to communities where episodes like these were part of the fabric of daily life.

Over the next ten months, the efforts by the communities to reduce self-harm by responding to the problems of boredom and unfulfilled ambition appeared to be paying off. There hadn't been any deaths, and episodes like these were decreasing in frequency.

On the plane back to Darwin, I sat next to Bob Beadman, the Northern Territory bureaucrat who had demonstrated strong support for the Tiwi community during the meeting. Despite the Burke Government's propensity to play red-neck politics, people like Beadman are evidence that, at a policy level, it is capable of embracing some changes that will strengthen communities. Beadman joined the Northern Territory Government in 1994 and has been involved in Aboriginal affairs at a senior level since 1973. His perspective on indigenous policy since the 1967 referendum was both informed and sympathetic. In something of a monologue, partly because of the difficulty of talking above the noise of the plane's propellers, he said 'The Government thought they were creating a welfare net under people. In fact, they were creating hammocks. The sooner that's addressed and the incentive to return to the workforce is created the better because we're in a situation of worsening social outcomes.' He described the late sixties award wage decision on pastoral properties as 'a principled decision because you could not continue a situation where Aboriginal stockmen were paid a third of what white stockmen were', but noted that 'the effect was that the excess numbers of Aboriginal stockmen were laid off. Their wives were laid off out of the kitchens at the homestead and whereas they were paid with a side of bullock here and a bag of flour there, the law required they were paid in cash and the industry couldn't stand it.'

There were other factors too, Beadman said, like the arrival of the beef trains and the use of aeroplanes and motorbikes for mustering, with the result that Aboriginal stockmen were sent off in droves, only to gravitate to the towns and become fringe dwellers 'with all the social pitfalls that accompanied that'.

'Then, in the middle seventies', he continued, 'there was the abandonment of the system of paying training allowances and its replacement with welfare benefits. Then came the advent of the grants-in-aid program, where massive new sums of money became available in the mistaken belief that Aboriginal communities were the last caring, sharing, communistic societies on earth, and what that created was a lowest common denominator effect. The able-bodied person with a work ethic laboring away in the sun for a community enterprise saw the lazy person sitting under a tree, and it soon became apparent that the fruits of the labor of the hard workers were going to be shared by the bludger. So the hard worker said, "This is a mug's game" and packed it in, too.

'Thirty years ago all these remote communities were self-sufficient in terms of vegetables and fruit and bakeries. Now, in the something-for-nothing economy, all of those small-scale enterprises have disappeared, with all the negative social consequences that brings.

'Everything happened too quickly', he said, 'with too little preparation.' As I listened to him, I thought of Palm Island and the words of Dulcie Isaro: 'It's just sad that the first thing that came into the hands of our people was the pub and the drink'.

It was some months later, after the football season and an emphatic victory by Essendon in the AFL Grand Final, that I met Michael Long. We talked about his parents and his own efforts to deal with the stolen generations' legacy of grief, pain, ignorance and unresolved anger. In February 1999, Michael had helped organise a family reunion in Darwin. Jack's older brother, Ted Carter, had managed to trace his younger brother and presented him with some of the evidence of his parents unsuccessful attempts to bring him home. Although many tears were shed, Michael Long said a lot of questions were answered.

'Most of the people who were there I didn't really know that well', he said. 'I met cousins for the first time, our kids met each other for the first time. Everyone arrived not knowing what was going to happen. I was nervous because I'd helped plan the day and the structure of how it was going to go. I did a video with Archie Roach's song *They Took the Children Away*. I didn't have much footage, a bit of my old man, a bit of uncle Ted. Everyone was teary-eyed because it was an emotional time.'

Michael continued, 'My father, I suppose, didn't know what was going to become of the day. For me, I thought it might have triggered something, the memory of what had happened. Dad always talks from the heart. He's a bit like me. And when it came to his turn to talk, he spoke of growing up without a mother. How it was horrible growing up as a kid. He doesn't remember being taken away. That's probably the hardest thing. That's one of the things he reinforced. Not growing up with a mother, not being loved or cuddled or hugged, or knowing that someone loved you, someone was there, knowing that you were safe. That was the thing that affects you. Without a mother and a father. A lot of things he didn't know: what happened, why it happened, why they didn't come and get him. He said the Tiwi people had looked after the kids, had taken Dad in, claimed him as part of their family, and he was very grateful for that. Dad grew up, a boy from the desert, as a Tiwi, learning their ways and their customs. Dad's a great hunter, knows so much about the island and the people and yet his own culture, the desert culture, he doesn't know so much about.'

The family gathered again in January for a barbecue, but the most important step will be to return to Ti-Tree. Michael is hoping that it will happen soon. The Long and Carter families seemed receptive to the idea at the reunion, but the emotions were too strong for Jack to move too fast. 'I don't think he wants to die without knowing where his own children and grandchildren are from', said Michael. 'Until he does return I think his mum won't rest in peace.'

After our conversation, Michael went to the newly-opened Museum of Melbourne to see the indigenous exhibition. There, he had a chance meeting with Max Stuart, the senior Arente man who was the subject of one of the documentaries at the exhibition. 'You are Anmatyerre', Stuart said without hesitating. 'I knew your grandfather Johnny Long and your grandmother Weeta Nampitjinpa Max.'

Long was shocked. He had only discovered the name of his grandmother a year earlier. Stuart also said how he remembered playing with young Johnny, Michael's father, in a rock pool when he was a toddler. Jack's parents, insisted Stuart, wanted to get him back, wanted 'to get that young puppy off that island'.

Chips Mackinolty

Starring in a leading film role as a child has not much changed the life of Sebina Willy (Bet Bet in *We of the Never Never*, here with mother Hanna and two of three children). Her daughter danced at the celebrations at Elsey Station, the film's setting, when it was returned to its traditional owners in 2000.

7 The Never Never: Us mob GO!

My wish is for the parents, uncles, those who drink, to say, 'Hey, this is a good thing. We can see the future now. I'm sick of standing here drinking every day.' Robert Lee, Katherine

The polarisation of this community, black and white, is one of the greatest enduring tragedies in the Northern Territory, because it's as bad now as it was when I came here 30 years ago. Bob Collins, Darwin

Sebina Willy was eight years old when she starred in a big-budget movie. She rode in an open carriage with Tamie and Malcolm Fraser, then Australia's prime minister, to the world premiere in Canberra, and she saw traffic lights for the first time. The movie was *We of the Never Never*, and Sebina played Bet Bet. It was shot on location at Elsey Station, about 150 kilometres south-west of Katherine. My sister, Sally Gordon, was the make-up artist, and when the project was over she asked the community elders if Sebina could come for a holiday at our family home in Brisbane, and then stay with her in Sydney when she resumed work. They agreed and Sebina arrived in Brisbane at the end of the shoot. She called our place 'Dorothy's camp' in deference to my mum.

I remember driving to a Chinese restaurant for my parents' thirtieth wedding anniversary. Sebina was still fascinated by traffic lights and became increasing hyped when we had a run of greens. 'Green! Us mob GO!' she'd shout. When our luck finally came to an end, her displeasure was transparent. 'I hate that one red. Him bin fuckin' rubbish!' The remark took us all a little by surprise and, much later in the evening, my father remarked, 'She's not too keen on those red lights'.

Down in Sydney, Sally used to start work when it was still dark, and on the way to one job Sebina remarked thoughtfully 'Your sun. Him bin tired.'

'I beg your pardon?', said Sally.

'Your sun. Him bin sleepy eye. Our Djembere sun, he always gets up before we do.'

There were other happy allusions to life at Djembere, or Duck Creek, which later became the community of Jilkminggan. And there was also one fleeting reference to the white politician who was said to have told her people to vote for him or their children would be taken away.

Before this journey, I had only been to the Northern Territory on the way to somewhere else, usually as part of the press contigent when a prime minister went overseas. I hadn't been beyond the airport. Now, I had the chance to travel extensively. The day after returning from the Tiwis, I took the opportunity to seek out Sebina, almost 20 years after we had met. I enlisted the help of Chips Mackinolty, a journalist, artist, photographer, screen printer and activist who was described by one AAP reporter as a 'long-term irritant'. He took it as a compliment.

Mackinolty had developed a special relationship with the Jawoyn people, and a high regard for Robert Lee. Lee was advancing plans for a regional authority that would represent and empower communities like Sebina's and have its headquarters at Katherine. My plan was to meet Lee and visit Jilkminggan with him, along with some other places along the way.

We left around dawn and had breakfast at Hayes Creek, a roadhouse run by a former policeman with an uncanny memory. Although Chips had never introduced himself or engaged in more than a monosyllabic pleasantries, his needs were filed in the computer of the former policeman's mind. Whenever he pulled in to the drive on the way back to Darwin, there were two cold cans of beer on the counter, takeaways for the trip home. When he saw Chips had a companion, he simply made it four.

Lee is a chain-smoker who was born in the bush at Barunga before they established a community there. He's been a truckdriver, a carpenter, a member of a travelling boxing troupe and a drunk, but has never been in receipt of government benefits. Now, with a still youthful face and a beard specked with white, he is the executive director of the Jawoyn Association and the driving force behind a plan to bring all Jawoyn communities within the proposed system of regional government. The essence of the plan is familiar: for the Aboriginal people to take responsibility for improving outcomes like 90 per cent unemployment, 7 per cent adult literacy and up to 50 per cent of the adult population suffering from diabetes.

On the way from Katherine to see Sebina, we stopped by two places that epitomise the Jawoyn capacity for lateral thinking. The first was Warlangluk, a 16-hectare property where a rehabilitation program to deal with alcohol abuse is being established as part of a native title settlement. The agreement was sealed in May. Then we visited Banatjarl, a cattle property Lee wants to develop as a diversionary program for juvenile offenders. It has the basic infrastructure of a farm, including a manager's house, but needs more buildings to accommodate up to 20 young offenders. Any more than that, Lee explained, and it would become an institution.

Unlike Sebina, the first city experience of many of Jawoyn young is when they are sent to jail. Lee wants this to change. He would like to see a pilot program where errant juveniles and young men are given skills in agriculture, trades and art, as well as drug and alcohol education. Aside from being an option for the courts, it would give communities the chance to implement their own justice plans.

The most audacious ambition is to develop trade links with the indigenous people of East Timor that would ultimately see a commercial trade in Australian buffalo. To this end, East Timorese would come to Jawoyn country and teach the locals, even the young offenders, how to domesticate the wild buffalo. It is an ambitious undertaking given the barriers of language and logistics, but Lee thinks it could be an international case study in reconciliation. Once it gets up and running, the aim is for a breeding herd of 50 buffalo to then be donated by the Jawoyn to East Timorese villages and, ultimately, for a trade to develop with East Timor and other parts of Asia. Not long ago, a group of East Timorese came for a look, and they spent a day searching for wild buffalo without seeing one. We were more fortunate. A massive buffalo was grazing barely 50 metres from where we pulled up at the property.

What distinguishes Lee's broader plan for regional government from some of the others is the pre-eminent role it formally assigns to the community elders, who sit at the top of a three-tier structure, above a regional authority and the local communities. As Lee put it: 'We need to have their blessing and they have to understand what we're trying to achieve so they are part of the whole system. We've got to make sure we don't destroy the land or get carried away with all our economic initiatives and thinking.'

'Through this agreement', he said, 'we want to paint this picture, not just to our old people, but to our kids, to everyone in the community. If we manage it properly, monitor it, we'll see improvement in education and health. My wish is for the parents, uncles, those who drink, to say, "Hey, this is a good thing. We can see the future now. I'm sick of standing here drinking every day."'

One of the biggest health challenges for the Jawoyn is to tackle poor nutrition. This is compounded by food prices often being 35 per cent higher in the communities than in Katherine, which itself has higher prices than the already inflated rates in Darwin. An element of the response has been an agreement with the Fred Hollows Foundation and a co-operative health food chain to base a nutritionist in the region for the next three years. The aim is to give people the will and the means to tackle the barriers to employment.

It was after midday when we arrived at Jilkminggan, a neat, 'dry' (alcohol-free) community well off the highway, and followed directions to the house Sebina shares with her mother, Hanna, and three children. I'm not sure quite what I expected, but the meeting was something of an awkward anti-climax. Sebina was shy and her memory of that brief interlude had faded, just like the small portrait of herself as a child actress that she retrieved from somewhere inside.

The house compared less than favorably with others in the community but Sebina seemed happy enough. She explained that she was no longer married and was bringing up Bianca, Scott and Veronica with the help of Hanna. I asked her about her time in Brisbane and she struggled to remember much about it. It had been a good time making the movie, she said, but there was not the slightest hint of regret that it had failed to lead to something else, somewhere else. Midway through our conversation, she disappeared inside and returned with one of the books from the spoken and written English course she was taking with the Bachelor Institute of Tertiary Education. Her aim was to secure a job at the local school or creche. For her children, she said she had three hopes: 'To go to school, keep their culture, and live here'.

Bianca, who was seven, was among those who danced when Elsey Station was handed back to its traditional owners in February, almost 100 years after it inspired Jeannie Gunn's autobiographical novel. Sebina chose not to go to the ceremony. 'I went fishing', she said.

On the way back, we stopped at Katherine to drop off Robert Lee, and I met Irene Fisher. She had been taken from her mother, who was in turn stolen from hers. Irene was working for the Jawoyn Association to improve health outcomes. Her mother was taken as a baby from her grandmother's breast, she told me, and taken to Croker Island with her sisters. When she was about 16, her mother ran away to Darwin on a pearl lugger. She married a Navy man after Irene was born.

'I was taken from her when I was about eight. Mum was drinking. There was a lot of poverty and alcoholism. Though I didn't appreciate it then, it came from her own pain', she said. Since coming up to Katherine and learning more of what happened, she said she could understand. Her own journey of discovery began about ten years ago, when an aunt traced the family through the welfare system and made contact with her in Melbourne.

'I can still get teary. When I was put into a home we used to go to a holiday house and I still remember getting the call that my mother had died. They didn't bring us all together, so I could be with my brothers and sisters. It was just like she never existed in a way. It's something I bottled up.'

It wasn't that long ago, Chips told me, that Katherine was a racist town. Now things were much improved, but there was still a long way to go. 'You've still got that division between white and black. The majority of Aboriginal people either work for their own Aboriginal organisation or become a public employee', Robert Lee had explained on the way back from Jilkminggan. The local construction companies did not take on Aboriginal apprentices, so they set up their own building company. There was still no Aboriginal policeman. 'It's crazy in the year 2000.'

Companies may well respond that there isn't a pool of potential Aboriginal apprentices to choose from, and they would be right. That is why Lee was pushing for a fundamental change with direct control by the regional authority for the employment of teachers, principals, doctors and nurses. He was also trying to build bridges and partnerships, engaging the police, the parks and wildlife rangers and the defence department to come to communities so the children can see there are alternatives and opportunities and role models. 'All they see now is police arresting people and a couple of weeks later they're in jail', said Lee.

The next morning back in Darwin I met Bob Collins for breakfast at the Cyclone Cafe. He promised the best coffee and scrambled eggs in the country, and the cafe delivered. Collins is a former opposition leader in the Northern Territory Parliament, and was a cabinet minister in the Hawke and Keating governments, but he seemed even busier now that he had retired from politics. He was seated in the middle of the cafe, and gave the impression that this was a place where he regularly came to think and to talk. He drank his coffee from a mug as I ate breakfast, and he briefed me on the review of indigenous education in the Northern Territory he carried out for the NT Government in 1999. It was a review that reported a crisis, with 'unequivocal evidence of deteriorating outcomes from an already unacceptably low base'.

The most disturbing finding was that 11 to 16-year-old students in remote indigenous schools were averaging levels of achievement equivalent to Year Two or Three. 'The stark reality is that many indigenous students are leaving the school system with the English literacy and numeracy ability of a six to seven-year-old mainstream child', the report said.

Collins made 151 recommendations, proposing a radical new approach to engage indigenous parents and communities in the delivery of services and a seamless link between education and health. Why? Because health problems like hearing loss through ear inflections are often the main cause of learning difficulties. As Collins put it: 'When you think about the fact that you're teaching a foreign language and 90 per cent of kids in your class have profound hearing loss, it's a bit of an educational challenge'.

The initial NT Government response was less than positive. After pointing out that his government had shown the initiative in commissioning the report, the former chief minister and education minister, Shane Stone, told Parliament that no single group of Australians had had more money, effort and resources committed to them than the Aboriginal people: 'The inescapable fact in all this is that 40 per cent of our education budget is spent on 25 per cent of the population'.

And the truth? According to Collins, Aborigines made up 27 per cent of the Territory's population but accounted for almost 40 per cent of the children in schools. 'So despite the huge additional costs of isolation and disadvantage, they're spending the same proportion on Aboriginal and non-Aboriginal students.'

Since then, there had been a more considered response, with the NT Government supporting the recommendations and announcing pilot programs to fast-track learning for hearing-impaired students, boost attendance levels and provide more teachers of English as a second language.

It was a start, but well short of the full-throttle, whole-of-government response Collins believed was essential. 'We know that a focused partnership by all the elements can produce a better result with outcomes measured and published', he said. 'It's simple to say it, hard to do it. But where it is done, it works.'

Months after our conversation, Collins discovered the already bleak picture he had painted in the report had deteriorated. A survey of a cluster of rural indigenous schools late in the year found only 2 per cent of Year Three students could read at the required level, compared with 5 per cent in his report. Late in October, Collins told the national conference of the Australian Council for State School Organisations in Darwin that if results for remote Aboriginal children in the Northern Territory became much worse, they would be 'too low to measure'.

Back at the cafe, we spoke about other indigenous issues on the national agenda, like the stolen generations and the mandatory sentencing debate, and the way in which politics is played in the Territory. While maintained progress had been made in some areas, Collins said the racial divide remained as wide as when he embarked on his political career. 'The polarisation of this community, black and white, is one of the greatest enduring tragedies in the Northern Territory because it's as bad now as it was when I came here 30 years ago. The mandatory sentencing debate demonstrated that.'

His experience with the review has only reinforced his view that education is the key to making progress. 'There's this great buzzword these days, empowerment. People love it, and it's not a bad word actually. I hated it when I first heard it. I don't anymore. In one word it sums it all up: people having some degree of control over their own lives. It's impossible to have any control over your own life if you're not literate enough to understand the system you're living in. To have any chance you need Grade Seven literacy and numeracy as an absolute minimum, yet Aboriginal people are leaving school routinely across the Northern Territory with the literacy of a Grade Two kid in an urban school in Darwin. You've got to encourage kids that it's in their interests to go to school. You have to demonstrate that there's a positive result at the end. The way you do that is use role models. Success breeds success.'

He was talking about individuals, but the same principle applied to communities and regions. I paid for breakfast and bought a T-shirt opposing Denis Burke's mandatory sentencing regime. I realised then that it was more than the coffee and scrambled eggs that brought Bob Collins to the Cyclone Cafe.

Michael Gordon

Olympic athletes Patrick Johnson and Kyle Vander-Kuyp were among many Aboriginal sportspeople who talked to and inspired the next generation at an Indigenous Sport event at the community of Mutitjulu, near Uluru.

8 Alice to Uluru: An uneven field of dreams

It is time for this community to come out of denial and accept the truth. Alice Springs is awash with alcohol. Meredith Campbell, Alice Springs

To be Aboriginal is a spiritual thing inside you. It's not how dark you are or where you're from, what tribe or group. I've had to hold on to that. Kyle Vander-Kuyp

Kevin Wirri paints pictures in the style of Albert Namatjira. He paints them of his country from the front of the fibro house he shares with nine or so others in one of the 18 indigenous town camps at Alice Springs. Wirri does his painting in the afternoons, when he has finished his work as a river warden for the Aboriginal council, Tangentyere. Often, the conditions for painting are less than ideal.

When Wirri arrived at Mpwetyere Camp in 1974, they lived in humpies and army tents. A decade later, when some houses were built, it was known as 'Vietnam' because of the number of police cars and ambulances attending alcohol-related violence. 'It was not a safe place for kids. A lot of men would get drunk', says Wirri. 'They would fight each other. Some of the women would get drunk, too. The kids would see all this. These kinds of problems we still have today.'

Once, when he tried to break up an argument, he was stabbed and ended up in intensive care. It was then that Wirri embarked on a campaign to clean up the camp. It has since won three tidy camp awards, and gone from being regarded as the most strife-torn of the camps to somewhere in the middle. Even so, police had been called to Mpwetyere more than 50 times in the five months before my visit. Alcohol is the biggest problem and for more than two years, Wirri had been pushing a local solution: to have Mpwetyere Camp declared a grog-free, or restricted, area.

I asked him why. 'To keep people away with all those problems, like fighting. Mainly fighting', he said. It seemed a pretty simple argument.

Last year the Northern Territory Liquor Commission rejected his

91

application because of opposition from an unlikely quarter: the police. The week before my visit, Wirri was back before the commission with an appeal, this time with support from the Northern Territory Aboriginal Justice Advocacy Committee. The police were back too, opposing the appeal. They won and Kevin has since filed an application with the NT Supreme Court for a judicial review. It's a course of action that could prove costly for the community, but Wirri believes he has no choice.

The case highlights the scale of the grog problem in Alice Springs, which was the subject of a community-wide survey in 2000. It unfortunately did little to settle a fundamental disagreement about how the problem should be tackled.

Published in July, the report by Hauritz and Associates recommended a comprehensive attack on a problem that was not confined to those who drink by the river or in the camps. In an introduction to the findings, Meredith Campbell, of the Alice Alcohol Representative Committee, wrote:

> It is time for this community to come out of denial and accept the truth. Alice Springs is awash with alcohol. Alcohol recovery services exist in the daily — and nightly — context of a war zone. Their workers, including the police, operate within the adrenaline of battle. Young people obtain alcohol freely, young women are especially endangered when they are drunk. Alcohol is in the workplace, is used to raise money for new school facilities and to get fathers along to fundraising events. Kids don't get to school because of ongoing chaos at home. Read the report. It's all there.

Based on quantitative sampling and interviews with focus groups, the review found support for limits to be placed on the availability of alcohol for the whole community, with 57 per cent of people supporting Kevin Wirri's campaign to have his camp declared dry. Echoing the Collins report of 1999, it reported that 'many children of Aboriginal background are not getting to school, do not have the literacy and numeracy of the grandparents, and few are getting to secondary levels. As described by many of the women in town camps, children are at high risk because of alcohol-related fights, family violence and disruptive nights/early mornings.'

So frustrated were some non-drinking Aboriginal women at Santa Teresa that they would use four-wheel drives to try to ram the taxis engaged by entrepreneurs to bring in alcohol bought from take-away outlets. Emphatically, the review found, the people of Alice Springs wanted the alcohol tap turned down.

Despite the strength of opinion reflected in the research, Denis Burke dismissed the recommendations as 'quite unbalanced, quite unscientific'. 'To my mind, the community could have been far more honest, and rather than suggesting that Alice Springs has a problem, they could say that there is a sector of the population in Alice Springs who are essentially itinerants who have a major problem in Alice Springs', he said. To many of those who took part in the study, the response was a clear case of denial, and an excuse for failing to act.

The police chief in Alice Springs, Commander Bob Fields, told me he admired and supported Wirri's efforts to combat the grog, but added that he had grave reservations about the proposed ban. 'Our concern is that the declaration of the place as a restricted area will not get to the core of the problems of Mpwetyere Camp, but it will give people false expectations that somehow things will come right down there', he said. 'We believe also it doesn't encourage any proactive or preventative strategies being put in place or attempted down there in terms of dealing with the issue. If the end result is that police continue to go there, but just under another guise of a breach of the Liquor Act, rather than an assault or a disturbance, we don't see that that's going to mean much.'

Fields said he was concerned that Wirri didn't have the support of the drinkers in the camp. He also feared that if the ban were implemented and police confiscated alcohol or even vehicles, the drinkers would turn their anger on Wirri.

His arguments were rejected by Christopher Howse, who represented Wirri in the appeal. In his final submission he argued that Wirri had the support of the camp and had been implementing preventative strategies against incredible odds. 'I wonder can we say the same about the police?' he asked.

William Tilmouth is the executive director of the Tangentyere Council, which has responsibility for the camps. He maintained that the police response reflected a typical resistance to Aboriginal solutions. 'It's a clear example of the other laws failing and Aboriginal strategies being ignored — strategies that work.'

One example of those strategies is the job Wirri does as a river warden. The job begins at 5 am every day and involves engaging those who sleep and drink in the river banks and getting them either back to their camp, into accommodation or back to their country. When it began there were around 500 people living in the river. Now it is around 35. Wirri doesn't want an argument. He just wants Mpwetyere Camp to keep getting better, to be a role model. One day, he would like to start an art gallery.

The last afternoon I spent with him, it had been raining for days and the Todd River had burst its banks. At Mpwetyere Camp, a group of residents were trying to get warm by a fire on the concrete slab that is Wirri patio. One old fella appeared to be suffering from pneumonia and was taken to hospital a day or two later. Kevin was trying to assert his authority with a trouble-maker who was drunk. When things had calmed down, he showed me some of his watercolours. 'Roughs' of his country, he called them. Not finished works. I asked if I could buy one and he said the price was $5. I gave him $10, and he insisted that I take two.

I had not intended to visit Mutitjulu, the community at Uluru. I hadn't written seeking permission or even made contact by phone in the preceding weeks. So it was hardly surprising that when I rang from Alice and asked about the possibility of calling by, I was given short shrift. I hadn't given sufficient notice, the woman said, quite correctly, and, in any case, Charlie Perkins was coming the next day with a whole group of Aboriginal sportspeople, and they were flat out getting ready.

I put down the receiver, looked up Charlie's mobile phone number in my contact book, and gave him a call. I had covered national politics for years and spoken to Perkins on many occasions, but I did not know him well. He was on the board of ATSIC, but in most of the big debates of the 1990s, he had been more of a peripheral player, a loud, uncompromising and mostly angry voice on the sidelines. Or that was how it appeared.

Charlie answered the phone and I told him about my trip and my predicament. He was polite, warm, interested. He wasn't going to be with the group, he said, but I was more than welcome to join them. I was to just ring Glenn Brennan and say it was OK with Perkins. Brennan was the manager of the Indigenous Sport Program at the Australian Sports Commission. I didn't know it at the time, but one of Charlie's last acts had been to play the key role in establishing the program and ensuring that it was adequately funded. Brennan was receptive, too, from the moment I mentioned Charlie's name.

It was early afternoon the following day when I checked into my motel room at the Uluru resort and went off to find Brennan. He was in the process of escorting about 40 promising indigenous athletes on to a bus, along with a group of elite athletes and sporting legends. There was Nicky Winmar, Evonne Goolagong Cawley, Tony Mundine, Patrick Johnson, Kyle Vander-Kuyp and Shane Gould. Many of the kids were urban Aborigines who had never seen the bush, let alone visited a community like Mutitjulu.

The community has a population of around 340 and is within a short drive of one of the country's most popular tourist destinations, but for many of its people it may as well be a world away. They have neither the education nor the language skills to compete for jobs at the resort. There isn't even a CDEP and unemployment is higher than 90 per cent. To reach Mutitjulu you pass several signs indicating that this is Aboriginal land and outsiders are not welcome.

Outside the bus, we were met by community leaders and invited to have a walk around the community. But for several minutes it reminded me of those awkward beginnings to dancing class as a teenager, where the girls are on one side of the room and the boys on the other, with no-one prepared to make the first move. So we strolled along, with the young kids peeping out from behind doors of dilapidated buildings. Then Patrick and Kyle approached a couple of kids playing soccer and joined in. What followed was a sometimes surreal cultural and athletic smorgasbord that lasted a couple of hours and centred on the basketball court and the rough field of red dirt: an uneven field of dreams.

The two athletes were just a few months from competing in the Sydney Olympics, but both were uninhibited and unrestrained as they played kick-to-kick and cricket, running aggressively between the makeshift wickets. Nicky Winmar played footy, too, but seemed withdrawn, introspective. He explained later that he grew up in a community just like this, in a house with corrugated iron walls and no floor, and he found watching the children deeply moving. Eventually, he drifted away from all the activity and made a campfire at a clearing near where the barbecue was being fired up. He said later he just wanted to warm up, but I suspect he wanted to bring out the older people. Within 15 minutes, he was joined by maybe twenty of the old women. They sat with him in a circle around the fire. The men came later.

The next morning at the resort, the sports stars sat in front of the apprentices and told their stories, one by one. Vander-Kuyp told how he was ten when he set himself the goal of competing in the Olympics. 'I can see a little bit of me in everyone here. Kids are aiming high, unsure, not confident. Am I going to get there? All of us have felt that.' Mundine told how he was born in Grafton and held nine titles. 'I haven't touched any alcohol, or drugs or smoked in my life and I'm still the same', he said. 'It's up to you what you put inside your mouth.' Johnson, who was brought up by his Irish father on a fishing boat in the Whitsundays after his Aboriginal mother died when he was two, said he was just starting out. 'It's all about getting there and proving yourself. There's no limitations.'

'You know my name's Nicky Winmar', said Winmar, when his turn arrived. 'But my real name's Neil. My father's name's Neil, from a place called Pingelly, two hours south-east of Perth. I worked as a farmhand with my dad at age 14. My dad was a shearer. I had a lot of cousins who were talented footballers, basketballers. I played a lot of basketball before I played football and I wasn't as good as them, but my dad trained me a different way. He trained me hard and made me more dedicated to my sport.' Winmar was the first Aboriginal to play 200 AFL games. He retired after

251. 'It's a tough road, but in the end I enjoyed it and I'm happy to be here to tell you about it.'

The experiences in sport contrasted sharply, but there was one common denominator for the indigenous champions. In every case Aboriginality added a dimension to that old sporting cliche: no pain, no gain. Invariably, the road to glory is marked by loneliness, isolation and, to varying degrees, racial vilification. The challenges are so formidable that those who meet them are often all the stronger when it comes to dealing with mere opponents.

Winmar was most qualified to speak on the blight of racism, having single-handedly put the issue on the AFL's agenda in 1993 when he lifted his St Kilda jumper in front of the Collingwood crowd, pointed to the color of his skin and uttered those words: 'I'm black and I'm proud to be black'. His message to the young athletes on racism was one of zero tolerance. There are heavy fines now for those who resorted to racial slurs, and they should be made to pay.

'Sport is now like a job in the office', Winmar explained. 'If somebody gives you racial abuse at work, you report it to somebody. It's the same if it happens on the sporting field. Tell the referee or the umpire or your coach. I don't care what your colour is, what race you are. If you've got the gift, you go out and give it your best shot. If there is someone out there ready to verbally abuse you, it's because you're better than them.'

Vander-Kuyp explained that racism in track and field was far less common, not least because of the domination of so many events by black athletes. Rather, he had suffered from it as a child, before his athletic ability transformed him from being 'Kyle the abo' at primary school to 'Kyle the athlete'. An optimist, he told the young athletes the barriers they faced would not be as great as for those who blazed the trail. 'Be proud of being Aboriginal. It's an advantage, not a disadvantage. Use it.'

Not everyone was convinced. Cawley recalled how she was seen as a novelty, the only Aboriginal tennis player. Then one young girl from Brisbane broke down and cried, saying it was 'really hard' being the only indigenous girl playing golf. There was no-one to look up to. No role model. Cawley offered comfort, saying the girl had plenty of friends in the room and shouldn't hesitate to call her any time. She also told her own story of racism in sport. She was playing doubles tennis at White City with her coach's daughter, and they won convincingly. When it was time to shake hands one of her opponents remarked that it was the first time she'd had 'the opportunity to play against a nigger'. Cawley was then 16.

The incident highlighted the need for mentors and support groups for indigenous competitors, something else Charlie Perkins had devoted his energy to behind the scenes. Cawley explained how two friends who worked in the Aboriginal affairs building in Sydney had helped her deal with her distress. She urged the young athletes to get to know each other, and form their own networks. 'If you have problems, call us. There's someone there for you.'

The discussion turned to the journey of reconciliation and how important it is on a personal level. That is when Vander-Kuyp told his story.

'I learn about the Aboriginal side inside of me. That's what reconciliation means to me. It's how important that link is inside you. I've never had it but there's something in there and it was explained to me by an elder that to be Aboriginal is a spiritual thing inside you. It's not how dark you are or where you're from, what tribe or group. I've had to hold on to that. Kids can envy me and think he's got everything, that he's done this and done that. But I haven't. I'm still empty, but I don't get down about that. That's what keeps me on track. That's what motivates me. Track's one small part of me and I've been able to do very well and have great success, but I've chosen a life journey and the next part of it is going to be my cultural side, my Aboriginal side.'

This will involve meeting the Aboriginal mother who put him up for adoption as a baby. 'She made contact with me in December last year out of the blue, without any warning', he said. 'Probably she wasn't meant to but she did it by phone. "Hi, Kyle, this is Susan, your mum." I'd known the basics of my history, but not surnames or anything significant. I knew her name was Susan and when she said her name it put me into a bit of shock, but also relieved me. I suppose I could feel her, and feel her voice, and heard part of me in her voice.'

Vander-Kuyp agonised out loud about whether this would happen before or after the Olympics. He said he operated on emotion every day, but this was probably a case where he should follow his head, not his heart, and wait. In the end that is what he did.

Evonne Goolagong Cawley told of her journey, too, saying she saw it as just as important as the other journey that took her to two Wimbledon singles titles. 'My dream since coming back to Australia [in 1992] is to learn more about my heritage and I've been doing that', she said. 'I've learnt more about myself now than I ever knew and that's been through getting with my elders, my teachers. I've had some magical experiences and it's given me a lot of confidence in myself and peace. It was something I'd been yearning for quite a few years. I'm fulfilling that dream, but I've still got a long way to go.'

And that's precisely what a great many people did.

Patrick Dodson, considered the father of reconciliation, put the question of a treaty squarely on the agenda before Corroboree 2000.

Michael Gordon

9 Broome to the Bridge: Half a bowl of reconciliation soup

The future is our future, if we have the courage and will. Otherwise, as the Irish saying goes, 'Bigots and begrudgers will never bid the past farewell', and we will be trapped in our history. Patrick Dodson

We, the living, still have much to apologise for to the living. Bob Carr

Denial of the hurt of the other is even more damaging than denial of one's own transgressions. Nelson Mandela

My plan in Broome was always imprecise, even more so than for the rest of this journey. Patrick Dodson had mentioned something about accompanying him to Fitzroy Crossing and visiting the community at Beagle Bay, a former mission. But Cyclone Rosita put paid to both ideas. I arrived in Broome five days after Rosita devastated part of the town and a number of the resorts. The power was still off for the majority of residents, and Dodson's house outside Broome was not even accessible by four-wheel drive. He had to wade through the water to his car to make the trip into town.

I had known Patrick, to talk to, for several years, usually as a voice on the phone. I was not alone in developing a high regard for the manner in which he handled his responsibilities as a leader of his people. Although he had stepped down as chairman of the Council for Aboriginal Reconciliation after reaching an impasse with John Howard in 1997, he is still regarded, rightly in my view, as the father of reconciliation. His is the voice of reason and there are very few in the country, black or white, who can match the power of his oratory. He has been a footballer, a boxer, a Catholic priest and an activist before he became a member of the Royal Commission into Aboriginal Deaths in Custody in 1989. In 1997, Martin Flanagan,

99

my colleague at *The Age*, had written of him: 'It is tempting to see Pat Dodson as a white person with dark skin. He's not. The truth is that he's an Aboriginal man who understands our culture a whole lot better than we understand his.' Flanagan was spot on.

Dodson is a Yawuru man, born in Broome in 1948. His father was white, his mother black, the daughter of Tailor Paddy Paddy Djagween who died in 1991 at the age of 111. The old man is buried in the Broome cemetery, where his tombstone bears the inscription 'Outstanding leader of the Yawuru'.

Although the destruction from the cyclone was still apparent, the day was perfect when Patrick and Paul Lane, his friend, aide and business partner, picked me up at my motel and drove to the old jetty where we spent a couple of hours talking over instant coffee. He seemed cheerful enough, but it was clearly a difficult time for Dodson and he seemed to be mulling over a dilemma. One the one hand he was bitterly disappointed with the progress toward reconciliation under the Howard Government; on the other he did not want to diminish the efforts of those on the council who were trying to get the best achievable outcome. A year or so earlier, he had put it to me as a metaphor: you needed the whole bowl of soup for reconciliation to be achieved, but if you were only offered half a bowl, you might as well take it. The rest would be pursued as unfinished business.

But how would he articulate this now? If he attended the handover of the council's documents to the people at the Corroboree 2000 event at the Opera House, it would be interpreted in some quarters as endorsement of an outcome he considered grossly inadequate. If he boycotted this event, but attended the people's walk across the bridge the following day, it would be seen as a slight on the work of the council. He was also worried that the event would leave those involved with a warm inner glow and even the wrong impression that things had changed. 'I think many Australians will think they've done something, but they won't be sure what it is they've done and be confused about why indigenous people are still concerned that there are matters of an unfinished nature to be pursued', he said.

In the end, he decided to give the whole event a miss, and lay out his position in a lecture to the Australian Institute of Aboriginal and Torres Strait Islander Studies a fortnight before Corroboree 2000. Our discussion on the jetty served as a kind of meandering prelude, reviewing what had happened and canvassing ideas on how the nation could ensure that progress was made.

You needed a hook, he insisted, something that ensured both sides accepted their roles and responsibilities. 'You're dealing with government', he said. 'You're not dealing with some church organisation that wants to do good.' The hook, of course, was a legislated framework of agreement or a treaty. 'In fact, you probably need a series of agreements and protocols in place', he said. 'Some of those are already in existence. Some just need to be better enacted or followed through and for someone to seriously have a watchdog role, someone who actually watches the stuff, some serious auditing and analysis of programs and expenditure at arms length to government so the government can be challenged as well as the indigenous people.' Someone like Allan Fels, the chairman of the Australian Competition and Consumer Commission.

But ultimately, an agreement also had to come to terms with history, and Dodson insisted 'the historical truth is far more complicated than saying whitefellas shouldn't have come here and blackfellas should have resisted'. On the jetty, and later in the lecture, he spoke of four broad divisions in 'our intertwined history', divisions that were not mutually exclusive. The first was the British instruction to take possession of the continent 'with the consent of the natives', an instruction that was never followed, paving the way for the legal fiction of terra nullius to provide an ongoing justification for reducing Aboriginal people to a disinherited and destabilised race.

The second division allowed for murder, the poisoning, the rape and enslavement of Aboriginal people. On the jetty he said this division encompassed Federation. 'Even in 1901 when the founding fathers came up with a draft constitution, the role of [Henry] Parkes and these guys neglected the Aboriginal reality because the darkest deeds were being created around them and they knew about them and may have even participated in them — and we've never really come to terms with that.'

The third division involved those with good intentions who were motivated by assimilation and salvation in their relationship with the Aboriginal people. It explained a significant part of the story of the stolen generations. The fourth period was the last decade and the formal period of reconciliation.

This period was never going to resolve all the issues in one hit, Dodson stressed. But it could have — should have — produced an agreement 'to work our way through complicated and difficult issues without seeing that as a threat to the coherence and unity of the country'. That was the real challenge of reconciliation.

The tragedy is that it this did not happen by the Centenary of Federation. As Dodson put it: 'It would have given great heart to many Australians, not just indigenous Australians, that we can relax in this country of ours, knowing that we all belong here, whatever the history has been, that we've come to terms with our demons and can have some pride about that'.

And whose responsibility was this failure?

'The big men in the country can rise above these things. That's what is required. You can have all the momentum you like out of the forces on the ground, but ultimately it will boil down to a small group of leaders who have to lead the country and the prime minister is, by virtue of that office, expected to be our leader, whoever he is. If you let the people down in that, you let the country down, not only yourself. I'm sure he worries about that. But he doesn't know how to get out of the bind that he's in.' Even amid his profound disappointment, Dodson could empathise with John Howard.

We left the jetty and drove past some significant places: the property in Mary Street where Dodson was born in the outhouse (there is a different house there now and his uncle Stanley lives there); the mango trees under which his grandfather used to sit; Kennedy Hill, or Mallingbar, where the Yawuru set up camp when they were forced into town (they chose it so they could still observe their country at Thangoo and look after it); the curfew area that endured until the mid-1960s; and finally the cemetery, where the inscription on his grandfather's grave sums up the philosophy that is his legacy:

> THE SUN RISES, WIND BLOWS, GRASS GROWS,
> THE TIDE COMES AN GOES.
> NO-ONE CAN EVER TAKE YOUR LAND.

Patrick Dodson delivered the Wentworth Lecture on 12 May, outlining the key principles that needed to be addressed in a legislated framework of agreements under several headings: political representation, reparations and compensation, regional agreements, indigenous regional self-government, cultural and intellectual property rights, recognition of customary law, and an economic base. If there was no agreement between the government and Aboriginal negotiators, the question of a treaty with Aboriginal people should be put to a referendum.

Though it was sincerely put, Dodson did not expect a positive response, and he included a scathing critique of the government's almost singular focus on what it calls 'practical reconciliation'. He said the government wanted to drive a wedge between concepts of rights and welfare and between those who advocated a rights agenda and those who sought relief from the appalling conditions. He said:

This is an attempt at a new spin on a very old wicket of divide and rule. If it were a matter of rice bowl politics, it might not be so bad, but it is far more sinister than that. It is about removing the centrality of community as the life centre and models on the individual as the essential unit of society. This is not our way. With all our social problems the answer is not to attack the foundations of our community by putting the individual before the community.

Dodson is most potent as a speaker when he talks in pictures. It is how he speaks to his people. He ended the lecture with the story of a pelican and a seagull:

The pelican gliding across the water is like the spirit of reconciliation, black and white together moving forward. The seagull is in some ways like the governments of the day, forever changing, coming on and off the process, flying off to scream loudly before one day returning and joining the voyage, navigating towards a new future. The future is our future, if we have the courage and will. Otherwise, as the Irish saying goes, 'Bigots and begrudgers will never bid the past farewell', and we will be trapped in our history.

The day before Dodson delivered the Wentworth Lecture, the Council for Aboriginal Reconciliation released the declaration that would be formally handed over to the people of Australia at the Opera House 15 days later. One member of the council was so incensed at the influence the prime minister had attempted to bear over the process that this person proposed to show me working documents revealing how Howard had made plain what was, and what was not, acceptable to him. But there was no need for a leak to demonstrate any of this. The prime minister was totally up-front about it — so up-front that he released a statement that night with the form of words he would have been prepared to support.

Originally, the intention was for this to be a declaration *for* reconciliation that would be endorsed by parliaments, but when Howard found several words in the draft unacceptable, it became a declaration *towards* reconciliation. The most contentious clause in the document was the reference to a formal apology, and in spite of

Howard's opposition, this clause remained, albeit in a slightly amended form. It said:

> As we walk the journey of healing, one part of the nation apologises and express-
> es its sorrow and sincere regret for the injustices of the past, so the other part
> accepts the apologies and forgives.

There was also recognition of 'continuing customary laws, beliefs and traditions' and an assertion of the right of Aboriginal and Torres Strait Islander peoples to the right of self-determination 'within the life of the nation'.

The prime minister's statement came within hours of the declaration being released, revealing that, despite 'extensive discussions', it had not been possible for the government to give its full support to the document finally adopted by the council. 'The areas of difference', his statement said, 'relate to customary law, the general application of the laws of Australia to all citizens, self-determination and a national apology as distinct from an expression of sorrow and sincere regret'. The Howard version recognised the place of 'traditional laws' within Aboriginal culture, asserted 'the right of Aboriginal and Torres Strait Islander peoples, along with all Australians, to determine their own destiny', expressed sorrow and profound regret for past injustices, and recognised 'the continuing trauma and hurt still suffered by many Aboriginals and Torres Strait Islanders'.

The differences were essentially semantic, but they were enough to ensure that the declaration lacked the weight it should have had and that the first day of Corroboree 2000 would be difficult indeed. They were fine words and noble sentiments to put on a poster and hang on the wall, but there was no commitment from the government to give those words legal effect, or even parliamentary authority. Many months earlier, when the first draft of the declaration was released for public consultations, Evelyn Scott had expressed the hope that one day it would be recited by schoolchildren in a reconciled nation. It did not get past first base.

So there we were, sitting in the Opera House on 27 May for what should have been a moment of national unity and resolve, but what was always instead just going to be uncomfortable. The last time Howard addressed a reconciliation forum, in 1997, he lost his temper and left diminished, later expressing regret for the way he had handled himself. This time he knew exactly what to expect and planned accordingly.

The first discordant note came from one of the elders who took part in the traditional welcome to country. Colin Gale challenged the prime minister to forget his own opinions and show leadership. The other contributions were far more measured, but they still left the prime minister isolated. Bob Carr, the New South Wales Premier, was perhaps the most eloquent, telling the audience:

> We are able to come together today because of two things: the resilience of the Aboriginal people, their survival from 1788 against all odds, and their generosity of spirit. And from their generosity and patience springs this great occasion: our last best hope for reconciliation.

Addressing the question of an apology, Carr said:

> Some argue that this generation can't meaningfully apologise for things done in our history. Yet even if we were to continue to relegate those things to a distant past, to write Aborigines out of our history as we wrote them out of our Constitution 100 years ago, we cannot deny the failures of our generation. And we, the living, still have much to apologise for to the living.

Carr also spoke of the area's haunting memories and powerful spirits, and the story of Bennelong, who made the first gesture of reconciliation and became, by turn, Governor Phillip's captive, houseguest, interpreter and prize exhibit:

> In 1792 Bennelong went with Phillip to England to be paraded before the court of King George III. When he came home three years later, Phillip's successor, Governor Hunter, reported that homesickness had much broken his spirit. He died discarded by those who had used him and rejected by his people.

The story of Bennelong, Carr observed, 'symbolises the tragedy inherent in our encounter over two centuries'.

Evelyn Scott, who succeeded Dodson as chair of the council, spoke next, expressing the hope that future generations would look back on the day as one of the landmark steps toward genuine reconciliation. Then came Geoff Clark, the ATSIC chairman, who concluded by directly addressing Howard:

> As I make way for you on the podium, Prime Minister, I invite you — no, I challenge you — not to speak about what you have decided for us, but what you will decide with us. Just one small step from you, Prime Minister, can be a great step forward for the nation.

It was a step he was not prepared to take. Howard spoke of the need to focus on the things that unite us and bind us together as Australians in the cause of healing wounds. But this means leaving the unresolved issues for someone else to fix. He spoke in turn of the 'wounds and divisions of the past', the 'injustices of the past', the impact that 'European civilisation had on the indigenous people', the 'mistakes' of the past, and finally of the 'tragedies and the sadness and the pain and the hurt and the cruelty of the past'. Yet every reference only invited the retort, delivered most forcefully by Charlie Perkins: 'Just say sorry!'

That afternoon at the Opera House, Mick Dodson delivered a speech that charted his life from his birth in 1950, and compared it with the life of the prime minister, 11 years his senior. His aim was to debunk Howard's assertion that the current generation should not be held accountable for the policies that caused injustice in the past. This argument remains the prime minister's main justification for opposing a formal apology. Dodson's contempt was obvious:

> I'm sorry for sounding as if I have a fixation with the present Prime Minister. This is one of the messages I wish to convey today: in fact the opposite is true. Our obsession with one man's incapacity to say sorry — the words he wants on a piece of paper — and the ruination of any meaningful apology with excuses and denial will forever distract us from lasting reconciliation. Let us not get hung up on this man's incapacity to bring himself to utter a simple human response to the suffering of others. It's not worth the effort and it distracts us from what we must do as a nation if we are to go forward in a true sense of reconciliation.
>
> The notion of 'practical reconciliation' is also a furphy. Although issues of the health, housing and education of indigenous Australians are of key concern to the nation, they are not the issues that are at the very heart or the very soul of reconciliation. But they are, quite simply, the entitlements every Australian should enjoy. The tragedy is they are entitlements successive governments have denied. Why should they be given some higher order of things in the reconciliation process? Reconciliation is about far deeper things — to do with nation, soul and spirit. Reconciliation is about the blood and flesh of the lives we must lead together, not the nuts and bolts of the entitlements as citizens we should all enjoy.

He concluded by endorsing his brother Patrick's call for a treaty.

John Howard did not take part in the walk across the Harbour Bridge the following day. He had made it clear from the outset that he considered this a day for the people, not the politicians. The government was represented by the Minister Assisting the Prime Minister on Reconciliation, Philip Ruddock, and the Minister for Aboriginal Affairs, John Herron. The Labor Party turned out in force, with Kim Beazley and Bob Carr among the early walkers and at least ten federal frontbenchers. Several Liberal MPs, including two junior ministers, also considered it appropriate to take part.

I was among those who set out early and, like the others, was overwhelmed by the size of the turnout and the joyous mood. On the way across I saw many national figures who had identified themselves with the cause, and many whose support for reconciliation had been a private matter: people like Murray Rose, the legendary swimmer. The breeze was crisp but the sky was blue, the perfect backdrop for a plane to write the word that Howard could not: SORRY.

It was early afternoon that Assistant Commissioner Dick Adams of the New South Wales Police conservatively estimated the crowd at 150 000, adding: 'Whether it was 150 000 or 400 000, you couldn't get any more people on the deck of the bridge and it was just a fabulous event'.

Gus Nossal, the deputy chair of the reconciliation council, said he had attended celebrations of the victory over Japan in 1945, and some of the biggest anti-Vietnam marches in the late 1960s, but said 'There is nothing that can compare with today'. Evonne Goolagong Cawley described it as the highlight of a lifetime. Scott, an activist since the 1967 referendum campaign, was overcome. 'I'll die happy tomorrow', she said.

But despite all of this and more, Patrick Dodson's concerns about the process remained well founded. There was clearly the national will to move forward, but how was that will to be harnessed? And how could it be translated into justice for indigenous Australia?

Before the Olympics, Nelson Mandela came to Australia to deliver the keynote address at World Reconciliation Day, an event inspired by a group of boys and their teacher at Trinity Grammar in Melbourne. Addressing a big crowd in Colonial Stadium, Mandela cited the walk across the bridge as evidence of a country 'wanting to heal itself and deal with the hurts of the past'. He could only 'humbly exhort' Australia to continue down this path, he said. 'Leaving wounds unattended leads to them festering, and eventually causes greater injury to the body of society. Denial of the hurt of the other is even more damaging than denial of one's own transgressions.'

At a luncheon in his honour, Sir Gustav Nossal had the task of welcoming the man who with courage, selflessness and grace had led the fight against apartheid in South Africa. Before I set out on this journey, I had visited Sir Gus at his office at Melbourne University, and he described his time on the reconciliation council as one of the most extraordinary experiences of his life. As a scientist, he could readily relate to the practical side of reconciliation, he told me. But he had also come to realise that the spiritual, or symbolic, side was just as important. It related, he believed to the very strongly felt need of indigenous people to be recognised as the first Australians, the nation's first peoples, the original owners and custodians of the land — a harsh and unforgiving land with which they had lived in ecological harmony for 50 000 years. As he saw it:

> They want Australians to examine the depths of the dispossession, to acknowledge the truth of Australian history. All right, you say, it was 212 years ago. But the fact of the matter is that they are living in the aftermath of certainly 150 years of institutionalised racism. It cannot be called anything else. So they inherited all the bad things that happened to Aboriginal people. They feel that very strongly, hence the land rights movements, hence the question of the stolen generations and the unfulfilled promises of the *Bringing Them Home* report, hence the desire to have customary laws and traditions respected and the strong feeling that they need to be valued.

One barrier to reconciliation was the feeling of a section of the non-indigenous community that they, too, were 'doing it tough' and were just as deserving of special assistance. Another was the stereotypical attitude many of these people had toward Aboriginal people. Said Sir Gus:

> I would be the first to admit that there are many Aboriginal people who, when offered a job, don't take it. That there are many Aboriginal people who cannot muster the discipline to send their kids to school everyday. But I think we have to tackle a problem like that with enormous compassion, with a bit of an eye to history, which has made things like that, rather than entering a 'blame the victim' mode.

Sir Gus clearly relished the role of preaching reconciliation, but was less comfortable with the political dimension of the task, particularly when it concerned John Howard's intransigence on the issue of the apology. More than once I had heard him describe his job, in the context of dealing with John Howard's strong views, as like walking on eggshells. Almost invariably, his approach was to applaud Howard and his government for the practical steps they were taking to advance reconciliation, and to nudge gently in those areas where he thought more movement was necessary. The approach reflected his nature, but it was also more likely to produce results.

His hand-written speech in honour of Mandela was one of the few cases where emotion had the ascendancy over diplomacy. With tears in his eyes, he concluded his address:

> As our young people learn the truth of this country's history, they will learn to grieve, to repair, to apologise and to forgive. This is not a black-armband view of history. It is the way forward, the way charted painfully and gloriously by Nelson Mandela, champion of the human spirit.

Pat Scala, *The Age*

Cathy Freeman, carrying the Aboriginal and
Australian flags after winning Olympic gold
in the 400 metres, became the touchstone of
the nation's mood in what were dubbed the
Reconciliation Games.

10 The Reconciliation Games: Part of a very special race

It was blackfellas reconciling in their own backyard. Stephen Page

We're gradually getting there. We just need a bit more effort from the whole of Australia, not just half. George Brown

All I know is I've made a lot of people happy from all kinds of backgrounds who call Australia home. And I'm happy. Cathy Freeman

Two months after the bridge walk and two months before the Olympics, Midnight Oil, one of the country's most enduring and influential rock bands, started a national tour at Papunya, the Northern Territory community that inspired the Aboriginal painting renaissance. More than a decade earlier, the band had travelled extensively in Aboriginal communities with the Warumpi Band in the 'Black Fella White Fella' tour. Now, one of the members of the Warumpi Band, Steve Butcher, was chair of the Papunya Aboriginal Council, and the Oils were keen to renew old friendships and, as Peter Garrett would say later, 'reground' themselves.

Shaken by the extent of petrol sniffing and other problems in the community, they spent some time at the school, talking to the children and the old people. Someone asked what they were up to and Garrett, conscious that their engagement as one of the acts in the closing ceremony had not as yet been made public, replied casually that there were a few things coming up.

'We're keeping an eye on the Olympics', he said. 'Might play, might not.' It was then that the old women turned as one and said, and not without pride: 'Oh, we're at the Olympics!'

And they were. Along with several hundred other desert women, they took part in the 'Awakening' segment of the opening ceremony

111

that set a reconciliation tone which lasted until the games were over. Only 11 minutes in duration, the segment represented a watershed in reconciliation for black Australia — the first time so many groups danced as one before such a huge domestic and international audience. 'It was blackfellas reconciling in their own backyard', said Stephen Page, the artistic director of the Bangarra Dance Theatre, who with Rhoda Roberts shared responsibility for the segment. Apart from being a source of pride and inspiration for those who took part and those who watched from the stands or on television, the event had practical consequences, exposing hundreds of urban Aborigines to their cultural inheritance. As Page told me later: 'All these Koori kids from different schools are going to do exchanges with the kids from Arnhem Land, so we're building our own bridge. We're not waiting for one little old fart to say sorry any more. We can't give our energy to that any more.'

For 34-year-old Page, the most emotional moment was a private one immediately before the opening ceremony, when he was invited into the converted car park that served as the dressing room for the women from the Central Desert to hear a hymn of thanks by those who had spent six hours preparing for the shortest, but one of the most significant, corroborees in history. 'To have close to 400 Central Desert women stand around you with their costumes on, ready to go onto the field — and all they want to do is say thank you — is pretty special.'

My own Olympic experience began in Melbourne in early September at the Prime Minister's Olympic Dinner, a gala black-tie event with a guest list of 2000, including many of Australia's greatest sporting heroes and highest achievers in business, politics and the arts. John Howard remarked in his keynote address that there was something marvellously symbolic in the venue, the Royal Exhibition Building — the place where the Federal Parliament sat for the first time on May 9, 1901.

'Here we are, back in Melbourne, the first Australian city to host the Olympic Games', the Prime Minister said, adding that it was also the city where Edwin Flack, 'our only representative in 1896', grew up and was educated.

It was a feel-good night drenched in sporting nostalgia, with Olympic highlights replayed in slow-motion to evocative music on a giant screen, and cameo appearances by living legends like Dawn Fraser and Murray Rose. It wasn't until shortly after we toasted 'the Queen and the people of Australia' that I sensed something was missing. Where was the indigenous presence?

It wasn't that the organisers intended this oversight. Far from it. It was just that the life experience of most of those present and the golden sporting era they celebrated reflected a time when things were different, a time when most of Australia was blissfully unaware that this was a country incomplete, when institutional discrimination, profound disadvantage, geography and racism consigned much of indigenous Australia to the fringe.

The Melbourne Olympics became known as the 'Friendly Games' for all the right reasons. But they weren't particularly friendly times for indigenous Australia. For a start, there was not a single Aborigine in the Australian team. Less than a year after those games were held, Cathy Freeman's great-uncle, Sonny Sibley, was arrested.

How symbolic was it, then, that Freeman, one of 11 Aborigines in Australia's team for these games, should be given the honour of lighting the Olympic cauldron six days later in Sydney? That the underlying theme of such a wonderful opening ceremony should be inclusion? And that, having confirmed her athletic greatness on the track, Freeman should run that joyous victory lap after the 400 metres carrying two flags tied together, the Australian and the Aboriginal?

If the Melbourne Games were a reflection of the country as it was then — a good-natured contradiction, egalitarian but blind — the Sydney Games amounted to a statement of how much Australia had changed in the intervening years, and a declaration of where the nation would like to go. If the criterion is potential for an enduring impact, these were the 'Reconciliation Games', and Cathy Freeman was their personification.

The decision for Freeman to light the cauldron — made jointly by Olympics Minister Michael Knight and Australian Olympic Committee President John Coates — was one of the best-kept secrets in the long build-up to the Games, along with the role the other distinguished sportswomen would play in the arrival of the torch at the Olympic stadium: Betty Cuthbert, Raelene Boyle, Dawn Fraser, Shirley Strickland de la Hunty, Shane Gould and Debbie Flintoff-King. Although Freeman was a fitting choice in her own right for the most important role, particularly as the Games represented the hundredth anniversary of women's involvement in the Olympics, the choice also had a reconciliation theme. It meant that the first and last Australians to receive the torch in Australia were Aboriginal.

Yet while it makes perfect logic in hindsight, it came as a surprise to most commentators and the public at large. My own concern about the choice of Freeman, unfounded as it turned out but probably shared by others, was that it would only add to the already awesome pressure already on this young athlete. Not only had she had to cope with the weight of favoritism and public expectations, there was the unresolved legal wrangle arising from her business separation from former partner, Nick Bideau. On top of all this, she had projected herself into the reconciliation debate, speaking out with passion on the stolen generations in an interview with the London *Telegraph* in mid-July.

Why had she done it? She gave part of the answer herself in the interview, saying it was important to her that she encouraged young people to believe in themselves, and for black and white Australians to start accepting 'each other's history', a history Freeman wanted a British audience to understand. To understand where she was coming from, you needed to go where she has been and look to her history, a family history that has absorbed all the negatives white Australia managed to conjure up, only to emerge resilient, strong and forgiving.

A starting point would have been to visit Palm Island over the weekend Freeman was competing. This was where Cathy's grandmother, Alice (Mero) Sibley, was taken after being removed from near Cooktown as an eight-year-old. It is also where Alice's second husband, Sonny Sibley, helped lead the strike in 1957. The story is told in Adrian McGregor's biography, *Cathy Freeman: A Journey Just Begun*. It was retold to the children of Palm during the island's first-ever cultural festival, a three-day event that began on Friday 24 September and was punctuated whenever Cathy settled into the starting blocks. Sonny Sibley, along with the six other ringleaders of the rebellion, was honoured at the festival as a hero who fought injustice and prejudice.

Among those who gave speeches on Palm was, ironically enough, Aboriginal Affairs Minister John Herron, whose submission to a Senate committee denying the existence of a stolen generation had been a catalyst for Freeman's stand. Herron spoke of the need for communities to take responsibility, and of the 'wonderful symbolism' of Cathy lighting the Olympic cauldron. He described the festival as a turning point in the island's sad history. 'I look over at the young kids over there, waiting to get on the merry-go-round, they're the hope of the future', he said. 'Old fellas like me and those of my generation have failed, there's no question, with the policies that were instituted at that time.'

If the experiences of her grandmother and the Sibleys gave Cathy an insight into the institutional racism that operated in Queensland until after the 1967 referendum, the story of her paternal grandfather highlights the blight of racism in sport that lingers still in certain quarters. Frank 'Big Shot' Fisher, was a champion sprinter and rugby league player known as 'The King' long before Wally Lewis. He so impressed a touring side from Great Britain in 1936 that the English captain, Gus Risman, wrote to him saying he was the best player they had encountered in Australia and inviting him to play in the United Kingdom. Because he was 'a controlled Aborigine' under Queensland legislation, Fisher needed permission from the Queensland Aboriginal authority to even apply for a passport. Permission was refused and, according to the account in *One-Eyed: A View of Australian Sport* by Douglas Booth and Colin Tatz, Fisher was told 'one star from Cherbourg was enough'.

This was a reference to Fisher's Cherbourg kinsman, Eddie Gilbert, the Aboriginal fast bowler who was given permission to travel inside Australia to play Sheffield Shield cricket, although the Aboriginal Protector refused to meet his expenses. Gilbert bowled out Donald Bradman for a duck in December 1931, and was subsequently described by Bradman as 'faster than anything seen from Larwood or anyone else'. But Gilbert's bowling action was considered suspect, and in 1936 the Queensland Cricket Association wrote to the Chief Protector advising that Gilbert's services were no longer required and asking that the cricketing clothes bought for Gilbert be laundered and returned. Gilbert never recovered. He died in 1978 from a combination of alcoholism and brain disease after spending 30 years in a Queensland mental institution.

Fisher was one of 11 children and his were the Birri Gubba people, a traditional language group embracing 18 Aboriginal tribes over a vast area of Queensland from the Whitsundays in the north, Charters Towers in the west, Marlborough in the east, and south to Clermont. He had 15 children, including Tollivar Fisher and Norman Freeman, Cathy's father. Norman was another fine athlete who died of a stroke at Woorabinda in 1993. Like Cathy's maternal grandfather, George Sibley, Norman suffered from diabetes, the disease that has increased exponentially in Aboriginal communities in recent decades.

As it turned out, Cathy Freeman comfortably handled the pressure of her role in the opening ceremony, even when the cauldron suffered a mild case of the wobbles before making its ascent above the stadium. This had something to do with the fact that she had attended a secret late-night rehearsal the day before and stayed until 5 am, when she considered everything under control. She also knew she had plenty of time to recover before the first round of the 400 metres.

On the evening of Monday, September 25, Freeman delivered the most powerful gesture of reconciliation in our history, providing a defining moment in the forging of a national identity that celebrates the unique heritage, culture and contribution of the nation's first people.

But before she did it, she did something almost as extraordinary, something that also marked her as a great Australian. She won a gold medal in one of the toughest events in athletics, despite carrying the burden of a nation's expectations for so long. Not since Ralph Doubell equalled the world record in the 800 metres at Mexico in 1968 had an Australian won an Olympic race on the flat. And not since 1968, when black Americans Tommy Smith and John Carlos stood by Australia's Peter Norman to receive their medals in the 200 metres — and gave the 'black power' salute — had such a strong statement been made on race at an Olympics.

However, Cathy's was a gesture of reconciliation, rather than defiance, from an athlete who has always worn her Aboriginality as comfortably, as naturally, as her smile. This was a statement of inclusiveness from a generous spirit, one she rehearsed six years ago at the Commonwealth Games when she first carried two flags. This time, she kicked off her red, black and yellow shoes and walked, jogged and danced barefoot, carrying the Australian and Aboriginal flags in a lap of unbridled joy. That her performance followed her lighting of the cauldron at the opening ceremony served only to increase the poignancy.

What her gesture seemed to boil down to was this: an invitation to follow her own example of pride in her own identity — an identity where family, Aboriginality, embrace of Australian values and love of country are distinct, but also serve to make the whole richer and more complete. She had lived it all her life and maybe this was the reason she coped so well with her own, as well as the nation's, expectations.

After the medal ceremony, the three place-getters assembled in the interview room and third place-getter, Great Britain's Katharine Merry, captured the mood when she said: 'I was part of a very special race this evening and I'm privileged to have run with Cathy in an Olympic final. I'm just over the moon.'

Freeman said she coped with the pressure by following her coach's instructions and by listening to the voice in her head that kept repeating: 'Do what you know! Do what you know!' She was asked what was running through her mind when she sat down on the track and stayed there for what seemed an eternity. 'Relief', she said. 'It was just relief. And I was just totally overwhelmed because I could feel the crowd just totally around me, all over me, all the emotion. I just felt everybody's emotions and happiness and joy just totally absorb into every pore of my body. I just had to sit down and try and make myself feel normal and get comfortable. It's very overwhelming just before the race and so to win a gold medal, after the race it was just beyond words.'

Ernie Dingo, the Aboriginal television personality, told her this was the hundredth Olympic gold medal for Australia, second Olympic Gold medal for indigenous Australia, and first for an indigenous individual. He then asked 'Is this what dreamtime stories are made of?' She struggled to answer it, saying all she knew was that her dream had come true.

Then a British reporter asked if she thought the symbolism of the two flags and what she had achieved could make a difference on reconciliation. Her response was immediate. 'I'm sure what's happened tonight and what I symbolise will make a difference to a lot of people's attitudes. To the person walking in the street, their attitude. Or to people in the political arena, their attitudes. All I know is I've made a lot of people happy from all kinds of backgrounds who call Australia home. And I'm happy.'

And who would she share the gold medal with?

'I'm going to share my Olympic gold medal with my husband and with my family, with my faaamillieeee', she beamed. 'I'm just going to go back to the loving arms of my family where I feel normal and I feel loved and safe and secure.'

In the stadium that night I felt the same sort of feeling there was on the Harbour Bridge, the feeling that something very positive was happening in the country. George Brown, a 17-year-old from the Wreck Bay Aboriginal community on the NSW south coast and who had danced in the opening ceremony, saw it in the crowd reaction to Freeman's victory. 'I couldn't believe how many non-indigenous people were holding up Aboriginal flags', he said. 'And the Australian flag with the Union Jack cut out and replaced by the Aboriginal flag — and how many Australians stood up for Cathy and cried when she went over to her mum. That was amazing.'

Amazing, but sadly not reflecting the mood of all Australians. In the letters columns of *The Cairns Post*, for example, there was a welter of criticism of the attention afforded to Freeman. 'I am sick to death of the media (*The Cairns Post* included) giving Cathy Freeman the special attention, like the Games were put on especially for her', wrote one woman. 'Queen Cathy — what a load of rubbish! She has won one gold medal. What about our other finer competitors?' Another woman complained it was 'such a shame that the reconciliation issue couldn't be laid to rest for two weeks while we enjoyed one of the greatest sporting events in history'. One man boasted how 'with skilful manoeuvring of channels when the words "Olympic" or "Cathy" were mentioned', he went almost a week without seeing anything about either.

It was left to Keith Saisell to argue it was impossible not to see Freeman's achievements 'in conjunction with the current soul searching of Australian society on how to best handle the reconciliation issue'. He concluded: 'We really are a racist society. Until we change we will always be the poorer for being like this. Come on people, it won't hurt to say "Well done Cathy" — no more than it will hurt to say sorry.'

The volunteers set the mood for the closing ceremony, just as they had for the previous 17 days, inviting those who arrived at the Olympic Stadium station to cheer their colleagues who had worked through the night to prepare the stadium for the evening's festivities. So we clapped and cheered as we walked, in a kind of warm-up for what was to follow. Then came the end of the marathon and a joyous finale to the extraordinary career of an unassuming champion Steve Moneghetti, who managed another top-ten finish, and who beamed through the final 400 metres. He described his final lap as a cross between a homecoming and a farewell. It was a night for partying, for Hill's hoists on stilts, for blow-up kangaroos, for prawns on bikes, for floating mirror balls.

But the reconciliation theme continued to resonate. At the rehearsal the day before, Savage Garden's Darren Hayes had approached Mandawuy Yunupingu and asked his permission to where a T-shirt emblazoned with the Aboriginal flag when he sang 'Affirmation'. Yunupingu was touched by the courtesy and delighted by the gesture. 'You'll be a legend', he said. There was never any doubt which song Yothu Yindi would perform. 'Treaty' is the band's anthem, written in anger after nothing came of Bob Hawke's 1987 support for a treaty in the run-up to the Bicentennial celebrations. When it came to the line about 'all you talking politicians', Mandawuy pointed up at VIP box where John Howard was seated. Then came Midnight Oil.

Before their return to Papunya in July, the band was considering a shortlist of songs for the closing ceremony, but was leaning toward 'The Real Thing', their remake of the Russell Morris hit. But as Peter Garrett explained later, they decided on 'Beds Are Burning', one of the songs on *Diesel and Dust*, the record that was a product of their experiences in communities in 1986. The chorus of 'Beds Are Burning' runs:

The time has come
To say fair's fair
To pay the rent
To pay our share
The time has come
A fact's a fact
It belongs to them
Let's give it back.

Back at Papunya, they also took the decision that resulted in them wearing black outfits with the words 'SORRY' written in white letters. As Garrett put it, 'We were struck once again by the resonant strength of the country, but also the extraordinary fracturing of communities that's going on there. So we felt that "Beds" had at least as much to say as it had when we first put it out, and that if there was one thing that was missing, it was the matter of the apology that hadn't been fully addressed by the Prime Minister and his Government. On that basis we simply resolved that we would wear "sorry" in some shape or form, and Gary [Morris] along with Martin Rotsey and Lee Frost, who has done some clothing for us, put the outfits together. She also made five black overalls which we wore for the sound check and the preliminary moment. When we were called to go on stage, we took them off and handed them to anybody that was standing around us and got up and played the song. We just went and did it.'

No-one was more pleasantly surprised than Mandawuy Yunupingu.

Ric Birch, the principal architect of the opening and closing ceremonies, insisted later that the reconciliation theme was the unconscious product of an attempt by himself and David Atkins, the ceremonies' artistic director, to deliver a message of inclusion. 'A defining moment in Australian history?' he asked, posing the question to himself. 'I'd love to think that the ceremonies will make Australia a better place for the forces of reconciliation, for all the forces of good in society. I'd love to think that would happen. But it's very much up to the audience and, ultimately, ceremonies probably reflect society rather than necessarily create history. What I hope is that it will inspire the people who watched it to move on.'

This aspiration was shared by young George Brown. 'We're hopefully taking the long road to reconciliation, but we're not necessarily half way yet. We're gradually getting there. We just need a bit more effort from the whole of Australia, not just half.'

Jason South, *The Age*

The year ended with another mass walk for reconciliation when a crowd of up to 400 000 turned out in Melbourne.

11 If not now, when?

The lack of consent and absence of agreements or treaties remains a stain on Australian history and the chief obstacle to constructing an honourable place for indigenous Australians in the modern state. Marcia Langton

The days of discipline and coercion are finished. What's left is incentive. Bob Collins

John, you've got to realise the job's not done. It's far from done. Charlie Perkins, on his deathbed, to John Singleton

This journey began with a hard question about what was the truth. It ends with one just as daunting: how does Australia respond to that truth?

As the nation prepared to celebrate the Centenary of Federation, there was another question, too. How does the country harness the spirit that manifested itself in the walk across Sydney Harbour Bridge and at the Sydney Olympics? The collective will to set things right was palpable at these and several other events in the life of the nation and it was reflected in some of the public opinion polls. Yet deep divisions remained about how this should be done, what the priorities should be and how long it should take.

When the formal process of reconciliation began a decade ago, there was an expectation that it would culminate before 1 January 2001 in an agreed document or documents of reconciliation. It might have been called a compact, or maybe even a treaty. What emerged fell well short of that lofty aspiration. The declaration *for* reconciliation that was to have been a foundation document became the declaration *towards* reconciliation and, even then, it was not embraced by the prime minister.

The Council for Aboriginal Reconciliation also produced a 'roadmap' for reconciliation, but there was no confidence that its directions would be followed. There were detailed strategies on how to address disadvantage, promote economic independence, promote the recognition of indigenous rights and sustain the reconciliation process, but from the very beginning John Howard made it clear that he had reservations about some of the key elements of these strategies, particularly in the area of rights. Although the council was anxious to provide a legislative framework for the 'unfinished business' to be pursued, the Howard Government was always going to be selective about what it was prepared to back. Patrick Dodson was correct when he said in the Wentworth Lecture in May that it was one thing for the council to make the strongest possible statements and recommendations, but quite another matter as to what government and the parliament would commit to doing about them.

In November, the Council of Australian Governments (comprising the prime minister, premiers, chief ministers and the President of the Australian Local Government Association) met in Canberra. Reconciliation was on the agenda, but most energy and debate were devoted to a national action plan on salinity and a demand from the states for relief from tax on petrol. The official communique addressed reconciliation after resource management, food regulation reform, quarantine restrictions, national competition policy and gambling. There was a 'thank you' to the Council for Reconciliation for its work over the previous decade and a recognition that the issue would 'require a concerted and sustained effort over many years'. Drawing on the lessons of the 'mixed success' on past efforts, the leaders committed themselves to an approach based on partnerships and shared responsibilities. The three priorities were to invest in community leadership initiatives, to review and rework programs and services to ensure they delivered 'practical' support and to forge greater links between the private sector and indigenous communities. The communique concluded:

> The Council [of Australian Governments] agreed to take a leading role in driving the necessary changes and will periodically review progress under these arrangements. The first review will be in 12 months. Where they have not done so, Ministerial Councils will develop action plans, performance reporting strategies and benchmarks.

If the communique had a familiar ring, it was because the very same forum had expressed remarkably similar sentiments at its meeting in Perth in December 1992, including a commitment to 'review annually progress in the achievement of improved outcomes in the delivery of programs and services for Aboriginal peoples and Torres Strait Islanders'. Despite this, and the promise of 'effective coordination in the formulation of policies' and acceptance of the need for 'increased clarity with respect to the roles and responsibilities of the various spheres of government', little was achieved. The 1992 'national commitment to improved outcomes' failed comprehensively.

Perhaps the biggest danger of assigning a leading role to this or any other group is that it leaves *the* leading role undefined. It provides an escape hatch for those with their eye on the small picture, for those obsessed with the political imperatives of the day. The lost opportunity of the ten-year formal process of reconciliation is that it failed to result in an agreement, where clear roles and responsibilities were assigned, ambitious targets set and a mechanism to hold the parties accountable agreed. We should have had our own kind of Marshall Plan, a plan that really combined the best thinkers, the resources and the political will in the pursuit of a common goal. What we got was a series of commitments to incremental progress in addressing disadvantage, admittedly many of them important: what John Howard calls practical reconciliation. We should have had a five-year plan, and realistically a ten-year plan as well, with goals clearly set so progress could be measured. What we got were a few commitments designed to ensure the issue stayed somewhere in the consciousness of the politicians.

The final report of the Council for Aboriginal Reconciliation, tabled in Federal Parliament in December, amounted to a much broader agenda than the one Howard believed was adequate. But what is to become of it?

The message from the council's work, and from the many conversations in the course of my own journey, is that any enduring resolution needs to be based on ten basic principles. It amounts to a ten-point proposition.

The first principle is that the ultimate leadership role and responsibility resides with the Commonwealth Government, and that means with the prime minister of the day. This is what Australians decided so emphatically in the 1967 referendum. It is also what flows from Australia's international obligations.

The second principle is that indigenous leaders must be able to negotiate from a position of knowledge and strength. The meeting of premiers with the prime minister in November 2000 was right to nominate investing in community leadership as its first priority, but part of this has to be building the capacity of community leaders to negotiate. It *is* crucial that authority be devolved and regional agreements encouraged, but without the necessary skills, particularly in the middle management areas, there will not be lasting change. Without informed consent, there will not be a lasting settlement.

The third principle is that while an agreement must be between the government of the day and the indigenous leadership, however it is defined, any settlement must involve all stakeholders, including the miners, pastoralists and fishing industries. If only government and representatives of indigenous Australia are involved, the support of the wider community for the process is unlikely to be sustained. This is particularly so because the issue of access and management of resources is so fundamental.

The fourth principle is that progress toward a compact between politicians, stakeholders and indigenous Australians must continue to be underpinned by momentum for reconciliation in the wider community. Here the work of Reconciliation Australia, the foundation to carry on with the work of the Council for Aboriginal Reconciliation, will be crucial. Just as important will be the willingness of the Commonwealth and the private sector to ensure that it is adequately resourced. And fundamental will be the role of the education system.

The fifth principle is that the key to achieving better outcomes is incentive. As Bob Collins remarked at the Cyclone Cafe in Darwin: 'The days of discipline and coercion are finished. What's left is incentive.' But how do you provide it? Surely, for instance, there could be a system of rewards for communities prepared to become self-sufficient in fruit and vegetables (as many were in the days of the missions), with additional assistance in employment and training programs in areas like eco-tourism and ultimately the prospect of preferential tenders and joint ventures.

The sixth principle is that the capacity to become self-sufficient and economically more independent varies greatly across the country, not least for reasons of climate and natural resources, but overwhelmingly because of the failures in health and education. This must be factored into any system of agreements. While the potential for growing food is real in many communities where there is plenty of water and rich soil, what about the desert areas where the drinking water fails to meet health standards? The great danger in simply providing opportunities and incentives to set up enterprises is that the capacity isn't always there to take advantage of them. Once again, indigenous people will have been set up to fail.

The seventh principle is that 'upstream' approaches must be given a higher priority than 'downstream' ones. Upstream approaches are about dealing with causes; downstream about dealing with consequences. This means more resources and effort should be devoted to preventative strategies. The dominance of the downstream mentality can be seen in places like Mornington Island, where the most impressive infrastructure in the community is the tavern, the police station and the hospital. The tavern is the source of many of the problems, while the hospital and the police station deal with the consequences. Yet there was no recreation centre and not enough support for those trying to generate programs for those who need counselling, or for the promotion of sensible drinking.

Part of focusing upstream is respecting indigenous languages and culture, and ensuring that outsiders have awareness training. This means that the indigenous health workers or education aides or police liasson officers are afforded the respect and consideration they deserve, and that is essential if they are to effectively perform their duties. This truth is presented compellingly in a recently published book by Richard Trudgen, *Why Warriors Lie Down and Die*. A non-indigenous man who has spent much of his working life with the Yolngu people of Arnhem Land, Trudgen argues that the primary cause of all the problems afflicting Aboriginal communities is the people's almost total loss of control over their lives. The aim of upstream strategies is to rebuild the capacity of people to take control of their own lives.

The eighth principle is that reconciliation is not just about addressing a problem or righting a wrong: it is also about giving white Australia more opportunity to share in the richness of indigenous culture and history. These, after all, are a central part of the nation's story and identity. It took the upcoming Olympics to make possible the Festival of Dreaming in 1997. It was the biggest celebration and exhibition of indigenous art and culture ever staged. Sandy Hollway, the chief executive of the games' organising committee, believed it would be a fitting legacy for such a festival to be held ever three or four years, but to move between the capital cities.

125

The ninth principle is that duplication is dumb. A concerted effort is required to avoid the waste and overlap that asserts itself in both the delivery of services and in the proliferation of organisations, programs and structures. As Noel Pearson writes in *Our Right To Take Responsibility*:

> We need to recognise the incoherence and irrationality of many of these structures — the overlapping functions, the conflicting roles, the inefficient scale, the inappropriate representation, the lack of coordination and the waste of limited resources.

He was talking only about Aboriginal structures, but the same can be said about structures from all levels government and non-government organisations.

The final and most important principle is that the objective of any settlement has to be two-fold: to settle the historical, political, economic and social grievances whilst simultaneously charting a new course for the future. The problem with the Howard Government approach is that it assumes the latter can be achieved without addressing the former. This is a formula for failure. As Marcia Langton said in her lecture, *A Treaty Between Our Nations*, in October 2000, these grievances represent a loose thread in the web of our civil society:

> The lack of consent and the absence of agreements or treaties, remains a stain on Australian history and the chief obstacle to constructing an honourable place for indigenous Australians in the modern state.

It does not have to follow, however, that everything has to be dealt with in one agreement, one hit. While an agreement that charts a course for the future must address the question of economic and political rights, some issues could be attended to in subsequent agreements, once the value of a process of formal agreements is demonstrated. Such an approach is consistent with the Howard philosophy on concentrating on those areas where agreement can be reached. A start would be to appoint a treaty committee, made up of government and indigenous representatives, to prepare recommendations for the prime minister on how to proceed. It may be that the final resolution culminates another ten-year process.

The temptation, of course, is to accept that it is all too hard, too intractable, too complicated, and to take consolation from the incremental progress that is made here and there. Yet the truth is that reconciliation is within the nation's grasp. It is happening in various ways in communities across the country and there are grounds for hope. As Professor Ian Ring, of James Cook University in Townsville, put it: 'We don't need to cast around for some new magic bullet. We need to apply the knowledge that's already there.'

It's just that it is happening so slowly in crucial areas that Australia's treatment of its first people remains a stain on the nation, a stain still damp with the blood and the tears of the innocent. When I made this point in an article published before Corroboree 2000, one reader considered it so emotional and overblown that he (or she) sent me a tissue in an unsigned envelope, along with the message, 'Pull yourself together man!' Yet it is the truth. The graves of children on Palm Island, the scars on the faces of women in Cape York, and the tears in the eyes of men like Jack Long, bear eloquent testimony to it.

One irony is that while John Howard has been a great disappointment on reconciliation, he, more than any politician in the country, has championed the principle of mutual obligation. This is not only fundamental to the idea of a treaty, but is an essential ingredient for programs which address the practical side of reconciliation. Moreover, his government has included several ministers who have demonstrated a capacity, even a determination, to make things better. Though it is seldom said publicly, Michael Wooldridge is widely regarded within indigenous communities as the best federal health minister Aboriginal Australia has ever had: courageous, imaginative and ready to back a risk. Without fanfare, Peter Reith developed an innovative employment policy for Aborigines that has produced promising if mixed results. Even John Herron, whose paternalistic manner has alienated many indigenous leaders, embraced a policy of regional autonomy that must be a foundation of any effort to achieve reconciliation.

Yet these efforts have been largely uncoordinated. Progress has been uneven and largely unmeasured against benchmarks. This is even more so with state and local government and the non-government sector. Will it change because of the last communique by the Council of Australian Governments?

The result is that for every good news story there remain many more examples where conditions are deteriorating. The number of indigenous Australians in vocational training is increasing, but so too is the level of domestic violence in many communities, the ratio of indigenous to non-indigenous people in Northern Territory jails, and the number of Aboriginal children in remote communities who are failing to meet the most basic standards of literacy and numeracy. How do you respond to the more alarming trends?

You start by endorsing a comprehensive, agreements-based strategy around the ten principles outlined above, one that seeks to magnify the things that have worked and incorporates the ideas that emerged from the Council for Aboriginal Reconciliation's work over the past decade. You elevate the Federal Minister for Aboriginal Affairs to Cabinet and assign him (or her) the task of overseeing the implementation of the strategy. And you instruct an independent agency to report annually on results, providing taxpayers with evidence that their money is well-spent. Within the Howard Government, Wooldridge remains far and away the person best equipped to oversee a massive task. (In a reshuffle of his ministry in December 2000, Howard handed responsibility for Aboriginal Affairs from John Herron to his immigration minister, Philip Ruddock, who was already in Cabinet and had been assisting Howard on the issue of reconciliation. But while the change meant the Aboriginal Affairs portfolio had been elevated, there was no shift in the government's approach.)

The central element of the strategy must be to empower those indigenous communities who are craving change and willing and able to take responsibility. Noel Pearson's partnership plan in Cape York is one example, but there are many others, including the Jawoyn people at Katherine and the Tiwi Islanders.

And what of the most dysfunctional communities, which lack the management skill to initiate change, even if the will exists? One answer is to engage those international agencies, like Community Aid Abroad, with track records of addressing these problems overseas. The report to Senator Herron by Colin Dillon referred to in Chapter Two advocated just this approach in respect of Palm Island and Doomadgee.

Another answer is to promote partnerships with the private sector and support organisations like the Lumbu Indigenous Foundation, the indigenous controlled and managed non-profit organisation chaired by Mick Dodson. Darren Godwell, the chief executive officer of Lumbu, maintained that it was simply impractical to look to regional bodies to solve the problems. Working on the basis of the 35 regions identified by ATSIC, Godwell asserted it would require 35 highly talented people to act as CEOs, 35 equally talented people to be financial controllers, 35 with big entrepreneurial ideas, 35 managers capable of building skills and capacity and so on. 'Frankly, mate', he said, 'we don't have half a dozen people that we can turn to'.

He also argued persuasively that a fundamental change was required in the relationship between the Commonwealth government on the one hand and state and local government on the other. 'The whole problem with indigenous affairs is that the Commonwealth-State relationship actually rewards the states for keeping indigenous people in disadvantaged circumstances', he said. This happened, he explained, through the extra payments that come through the Commonwealth grants commission. 'You get to make an argument that because you have a large indigenous population that's at such a disadvantage, you deserve larger pieces of the pie as special funding to tackle those issues. But there's no reward contingent upon achieving better outcomes. In fact the reward is the exact opposite.' A recent example was the Northern Territory Government being provided with extra funds for police because of its failure to provide diversionary programs for those young men convicted under its mandatory sentencing laws. The answer, according to Godwell, was for the Commonwealth to exercise the authority it was given in 1967 and take control.

But this is only one element of the solution. Another is for the non-government sector to become formalised and strengthened, with foundations like Lumbu working in a co-ordinated way with other bodies and companies like Normandy Mining and Rio Tinto, which have developed imaginative policies to promote indigenous employment. One valuable link between the government and the non-government sector would be to have a national steering committee to regularly review progress and offer advice, made up of respected figures from all sides of politics, business, the arts, sport and the non-government sector as well as the pastoral, mining and fishing industries.

Most importantly, though, a national strategy has to recognise that the longer the country disregards the emotional and spiritual questions that lie at the heart of Aboriginal life, the greater the cost will be of solving the crises in health and education. This is where Howard's failure has been manifest. His government's assertion to a Senate inquiry that there was no stolen generation was simply the latest, and the most hurtful, of a succession of episodes that either stalled or set back the process. There was outright denial (they weren't stolen), rationalisation (it was done with good intent) and finally trivialisation (it was no more than 10 per cent).

Some have suggested Howard's approach has a lot to do with him being a poll-driven prime minister. I have never accepted this. Rather, I consider him one of the most blinkered leaders Australia has had. He can be astute, brave, confident and even compassionate within his paradigm of social conservatism and economic rationalism. But he is uncomfortable and defensive outside it. His views on indigenous Australia are his own, and it is largely a politically convenient coincidence that they are shared by many Australians.

The difference between Howard and those he is supposed to lead, however, is that the prime minister has had access to the whole story. His government has received many of the reports outlining the problems and possible solutions. He has heard the trauma of the stolen generations first-hand. At his only visit to an indigenous community, he witnessed ceremonies no other political leader had been privileged to see. He talks of the 'black arm-band' view of history, but he knows the facts. There is no excuse for his blindness.

Good leaders, and great ones, are more often remembered for their responses to the unforeseen than the ideas they initiate. Howard's response to the Port Arthur massacre in 1996 was the introduction of national gun law reform — and he demonstrated courage, conviction and determination. The tragedy of his failure on indigenous issues has been that it coincided with an historic opportunity to achieve a sound basis for reconciliation. Several times on my journey, I encountered Aboriginal people who simply could not fathom how he could be so courageous on guns and so inadequate on race; how he could be so affronted by human rights abuses in East Timor, but so blind to them at home.

Would he change? Sir Gustav Nossal suggested in 1999 that Howard was on his own journey of reconciliation. But as his fifth year in office was coming to an end, there was little evidence that he had moved very far at all. He continued to reject the idea of a formal apology, opposed a formal agreement or treaty and refused to embrace words like 'self-determination' or the phrase that Aborigines and Torres Strait Islanders were the 'original owners and custodians of the land'. Howard defended his position on the apology and a treaty in part by saying that 'most Australians' agreed with him. The polls vindicated him on the apology, but would the people have a different view if the nation's leader was advocating one?

Before Corroboree 2000, Howard told an interviewer his views on reconciliation had changed and would continue to do so. At the end of June, I asked him to cite an example of where the change had taken place. 'I guess I'm even more strongly of the view that doing practical things are of benefit', he said. He agreed that symbolic acts were important, but bemoaned the tendency for the goal posts to keep being moved. The statement of 'sincere regret' made in Federal Parliament before Corroboree 2000 was a significant movement from the government's position a couple of years earlier, he said, but then there were demands for it to go further. There was more the government would do in the area of 'practical' reconciliation, he said, and there was no doubting his commitment. But he questioned the need for more legislation ('Legislation to do what?') and expressed disappointment that 'the treaty thing' had come back on the agenda.

I put it to him that, with the benefit of hindsight, he would have had a different position on the apology, but that there was now no point in changing because one section of the community would think him insincere, while another would regard it as a betrayal.

'That view is erroneous', he said. 'I've always conscientiously held the view I express. But I think that analysis is also correct ... If you say to me would I have handled it differently, my answer is no. In hindsight, one thing I would have done differently in '97 was not to have reacted angrily' (meaning at the reconciliation convention in Melbourne). Incidentally, he added, it wasn't the people turning their backs on him that made him lose his temper. It was the interjections when he was trying to explain his position on native title. 'I quite conscientiously hold the view that I've expressed on the formal apology ... So for both genuine and practical reasons, I won't be shifting my position.'

Clearly, the question of a formal apology and treaty will not be resolved until there is another prime minister. Even then, it would require a leader of commitment, strength and daring.

The final report of the Council for Aboriginal Reconciliation was handed over at a breakfast at Parliament House on 7 December

2000, four days after a crowd estimated at between 150 000 and 400 000 had joined in Melbourne's walk for reconciliation. There were just six recommendations, all of them designed to advance the roadmap for reconciliation and the declaration launched at Corroboree 2000 in Sydney. The final recommendation called on the Commonwealth Parliament to enact legislation 'to put in place a process which will unite all Australians by way of an agreement, or treaty, through which unresolved issues of reconciliation can be resolved'. What it amounted to, said council chair Evelyn Scott, was a call for a conversation about a treaty.

Howard responded by telling the gathering that reconciliation was now an 'unstoppable force', but he quickly indicated his views on a treaty were unchanged. Kim Beazley was more positive, saying: 'We must look into each other's eyes and find a way to implement the recommendations of this report'. But there was also a qualification: 'If there is a will for a lasting settlement, including a treaty or treaties, we must find a way'. If Beazley was going to a champion of the reconciliation cause, it would be after he became prime minister, not before.

Sir Gustav Nossal displayed his capacity for combining realism and optimism when he told the breakfast how serving on the council had been a life-changing experience:

> For a crusty old scientist, used to dealing with facts and hard data, clear analytical solutions, crisp indicators of success or failure, it was also quite an emotional experience as the realisation dawned that our quest for reconciliation must be a continuing struggle for the hearts and minds of all Australians, with no simple technological fixes, no Einsteinian flashes of right or wrong. Yet, untidy as the field is, no issue is of greater importance as we come to the centenary of federation.

He concluded with these words: 'The tidal wave which is reconciliation will come to shore as our young people learn the truths of our shared histories, freeing them to live in harmony in our shared land, Australia'.

In the course of the last year, I asked many people how quickly things might change if a whole-of-government approach was adopted, backed by the weight of unfettered prime ministerial support. The answer varied from 'years' to 'generations', with general agreement that there is no 'quick fix'.

But perhaps the more relevant question is this: what further price will be paid by indigenous Australians, and what more damage will be done to the nation, if we cannot collectively muster the wit and the will to give true reconciliation our best shot? How many more indigenous leaders will lament on their deathbed, as Charlie Perkins did before he died in October, that there is still so much more to be done?

Evelyn Scott, chair of the Council for Aboriginal Reconciliation, presented Prime Minister John Howard with the council's final report in December 2000.

Paul Harris, *The Age*

Australian Declaration Towards Reconciliation

We, the peoples of Australia, of many origins as we are, make a commitment to go on together in a spirit of reconciliation.

We value the unique status of Aboriginal and Torres Strait Islander peoples as the original owners and custodians of lands and waters.

We recognise this land and its waters were settled as colonies without treaty or consent.

Reaffirming the human rights of all Australians, we respect and recognise continuing customary laws, beliefs and traditions.

Through understanding the spiritual relationship between the land and its first peoples, we share our future and live in harmony.

Our nation must have the courage to own the truth, to heal the wounds of its past so that we can move on together at peace with ourselves.

Reconciliation must live in the hearts and minds of all Australians. Many steps have been taken, many steps remain as we learn our shared histories.

As we walk the journey of healing, one part of the nation apologises and expresses its sorrow and sincere regret for the injustices of the past, so the other part accepts the apologies and forgives.

We desire a future where all Australians enjoy their rights, accept their responsibilities, and have the opportunity to achieve their full potential.

And so, we pledge ourselves to stop injustice, overcome disadvantage, and respect that Aboriginal and Torres Strait Islander peoples have the right to self-determination within the life of the nation.

Our hope is for a united Australia that respects this land of ours; values the Aboriginal and Torres Strait Islander heritage; and provides justice and equity for all.

Drafted by the Council for Aboriginal Reconciliation, 2000

References

Aboriginal and Torres Strait Islander Women's Task Force on Violence Report, chairperson Boni Robertson, 1999

Bringing Them Home, report of the National Inquiry into the Separation of Aboriginal and Torres Strait Islander Children from their Families, April 1997

Context of Silence: Violence and the Remote Area Nurse, report prepared by the Faculty of Health Science, Central Queensland University, Rockhampton

National Commitment to Improved Outcomes in the Delivery of Programs and Services for Aboriginal Peoples and Torres Strait Islanders, endorsed by the Council of Australian Governments, 7 December 1992

Research into Issues Related to a Document of Reconciliation, report no 2, prepared for the Council for Aboriginal Reconciliation, Irving Saulwick and Associates with Denis Muller and Associates

Buku-Larrngay Mulka Centre, Saltwater, *Yirrkala Bark Paintings of Sea Country*, in association with Jennifer Isaacs Publishing, 1999

Douglas Booth and Colin Tatz, *One-Eyed: A View of Australian Sport*, Allen and Unwin, 2000

Bob Collins, *Learning Lessons: An Independent Review of Indigenous Education in the Northern Territory*, Northern Territory Department of Education, 1999

Coroners' Court, Darwin, findings in inquest of four people on the Tiwi Islands, nos 9817541; 9817544; 9823271; 9825948

Council for Aboriginal Reconciliation, *Reconciliation: Australia's Challenge*, final report of the council to the Prime Minister and the Commonwealth Parliament, December 2000

Council of Australian Governments, communique, Canberra, 3 October 2000

Patrick Dodson, *Beyond the Mourning Gate: Dealing with Unfinished Business*, Wentworth Lecture, Australian Institute of Aboriginal and Torres Strait Islander Studies, 12 May 2000

Geoff Genever, *Aborigines, Alcohol and Government Initiatives: A Report on the History and Effects of Alcohol Abuse in Cape York Aboriginal Communities*, Apunipima Cape York Health Council, 2000

——, *"Yes, but I never hit her in the face": A Survey of Attitudes to Domestic Violence in Cape York Aboriginal Communities*, Apunimipa Cape York Health Council, 2000

MA Hauritz, G McIlwain, F Finnsson, *Dollars Made From Broken Spirits*, report for the Northern Territory Government and Alice Springs Town Council, July 2000

Rosalind Kidd, *The Way We Civilise*, University of Queensland Press, 1997

Marcia Langton, *A Treaty Between Our Nations*, inaugural professorial lecture, University of Melbourne, 19 October 2000

Adrian McGregor, *Cathy Freeman: A Journey Just Begun*, Random House Australia, 1998

Noel Pearson, *Our Right To Take Responsibility*, Noel Pearson and Associates, 2000

Henry Reynolds, *Why Weren't We Told?*, Viking Penguin Books, 1999

———, *This Whispering in Our Hearts*, Allen and Unwin, 1998

Tim Rowse, *Obliged To Be Difficult*, Cambridge University Press, 2000

Richard Trudgen, *Why Warriors Lie Down And Die: Towards an Understanding of Why the Aboriginal People of Arnhem Land Face the Greatest Crisis in Health and Education Since European Contact*, Aboriginal Resource and Development Services, Darwin, 2000

Wadjularbinna, *Report on the Incidents at Doomadgee Communitry on November 19 1999 Onwards*

Galarrwuy Yunupingu, *We Know These Things To Be True*, Third Vincent Lingiari Memorial Lecture, 20 August 1998

Index